THE COMIC BOOK BIBLE

Written and Illustrated by
Rob Suggs

Coloring by
Christopher "Scribble Boy" Gray

BARBOUR
PUBLISHING

© 1995 by Screaming Communications.

ISBN 978-1-60260-685-2

All Scripture quotations are from The King James Version of the Bible.

Published by Barbour Publishing, Inc., P.O. Box 719, Uhrichsville, Ohio 44683
www.barbourbooks.com

*Our mission is to publish and distribute inspirational products offering exceptional
value and biblical encouragement to the masses.*

Member of the
Evangelical Christian
Publishers Association

Printed in India.

THE COMIC BOOK BIBLE

TABLE OF CONTENTS

THE OLD TESTAMENT

TABLE OF CONTENTS

THE NEW TESTAMENT

MAPS AND SPECIAL FEATURES

THE STORY OF CREATION

IN THE BEGINNING GOD CREATED THE HEAVEN AND THE EARTH. AND THE
EARTH WAS WITHOUT FORM, AND VOID; . . . .
GENESIS 1:1, 2

IN THE BEGINNING, GOD
CREATED EVERYTHING. THE
EARTH WAS EMPTY AND FORMLESS.

DARKNESS WAS EVERYWHERE, AND GOD'S SPIRIT HOVERED OVER THE WATERS.

AND DARKNESS WAS UPON THE FACE OF THE DEEP. AND THE SPIRIT OF GOD MOVED UPON THE FACE OF THE WATERS.
GENESIS 1:2

AND GOD SAID, "LET THERE BE LIGHT!"

HE CALLED THE LIGHT "DAY," AND THE DARKNESS "NIGHT." EVENING AND MORNING: THE FIRST DAY!

ON THE SECOND DAY, HE CREATED THE SKY AND THE CLOUDS.

THEN HE FILLED THE EARTH WITH GRASS, TREES, AND FLOWERS ON THE THIRD DAY.

The Story of Creation - Genesis 1 and 2

AND GOD SAID, LET THERE BE LIGHTS IN THE FIRMAMENT
OF THE HEAVEN TO DIVIDE THE DAY FROM THE NIGHT; . . . .
GENESIS 1:14

ON THE FOURTH DAY, HE MADE THE SUN, THE MOON, AND THE STARS
FOR LIGHT — AND TO MARK THE SEASONS.

ON THE FIFTH DAY, HE FILLED THE
WATERS WITH LIVING THINGS, AND
THE SKIES WITH BIRDS.

ON THE SIXTH DAY, HE MADE ALL
THE ANIMALS OF THE EARTH.
BUT ONE THING WAS STILL MISSING.

The Story of Creation - Genesis 1 and 2

AND GOD SAID, LET US MAKE MAN IN OUR IMAGE, AFTER OUR LIKENESS:
AND LET THEM HAVE DOMINION. . .OVER ALL
THE EARTH . . . .   GENESIS 1:26

IN HIS OWN LIKENESS, HE CREATED THE FIRST MAN AND THE FIRST WOMAN: ADAM AND EVE.

THEY WERE TO TEND THEIR BEAUTIFUL GARDEN, EDEN, AND TO NAME AND CARE FOR ALL THE ANIMALS.

THEN IT WAS THE SEVENTH DAY — AND GOD RESTED.

The Story of Creation - Genesis 1 and 2

THE STORY OF ADAM AND EVE

AND GOD SAID, BEHOLD, I HAVE GIVEN YOU EVERY HERB BEARING SEED,
. . . AND EVERY TREE; . . . TO YOU IT SHALL BE FOR MEAT.

GENESIS 1:29

... AND HE [THE SERPENT] SAID UNTO THE WOMAN, YEA, HATH GOD SAID, YE SHALL NOT EAT OF EVERY TREE OF THE GARDEN?   GENESIS 3:1

The Story of Adam and Eve - Genesis 3 and 4

... AND ADAM AND HIS WIFE HID THEMSELVES FROM THE
PRESENCE OF THE LORD GOD AMONGST THE TREES
OF THE GARDEN.   GENESIS 3:8

The Story of Adam and Eve - Genesis 3 and 4

... AND THE LORD HAD RESPECT UNTO ABEL AND TO HIS OFFERING: BUT UNTO CAIN AND TO HIS OFFERING HE HAD NOT RESPECT .... GENESIS 4:4-5

The Story of Adam and Eve - Genesis 3 and 4

THE STORY OF NOAH

AND GOD SAID UNTO NOAH ... MAKE THEE AN ARK OF GOPHER WOOD; ... AND OF EVERY LIVING OF ALL FLESH, TWO OF EVERY SORT SHALT THOU BRING INTO THE ARK .... GENESIS 6:13, 19

THUS DID NOAH; ACCORDING TO ALL THAT GOD
COMMANDED HIM, SO DID HE.   GENESIS 6:22

THERE WENT IN TWO AND TWO UNTO NOAH INTO THE ARK,
... AND IT CAME TO PASS AFTER SEVEN DAYS, THAT THE WATERS OF THE
FLOOD WERE UPON THE EARTH.   GENESIS 7:9-10

The Story of Noah - Genesis 6 and 7

AND GOD SPAKE UNTO NOAH, SAYING, GO FORTH OF THE ARK, THOU,
AND THY WIFE, AND THY SONS, AND THY SONS' WIVES WITH THEE.
GENESIS 8:15-16

THE DOVE RETURNED. NOAH RELEASED ANOTHER.

AN OLIVE BRANCH? THERE MUST BE A FEW TREE TOPS SHOWING!

FINALLY...

FATHER'S THIRD DOVE NEVER RETURNED! LOOKS LIKE WE'RE HEADED FOR DRY LAND!

ALL THE EVIL IS WASHED AWAY — AND NOW IT'S UP TO US TO START OVER!

O LORD, OUR FAMILY BEGINS THIS NEW LIFE WORSHIPING YOU!

THIS IS A RAINBOW: GOD'S REMINDER THAT HE WILL NEVER SEND ANOTHER FLOOD!

The Story of Noah - Genesis 6 and 7

THE STORY OF ABRAHAM

NOW THE LORD HAD SAID UNTO ABRAM, GET THEE OUT OF THY COUNTRY, AND FROM THY KINDRED, AND FROM THY FATHER'S HOUSE, UNTO A LAND THAT I WILL SHEW THEE.   GENESIS 12:1

GENERATIONS AFTER NOAH, GOD SPOKE TO A MAN NAMED ABRAHAM.

ABRAM, LEAVE YOUR COUNTRY, YOUR PEOPLE, AND YOUR FAMILY, AND GO TO THE LAND I WILL SHOW YOU.
YOU WILL BE THE FIRST OF A GREAT NATION, AND I WILL BLESS YOU. I WILL MAKE YOUR NAME GREAT, AND YOU WILL BE A BLESSING TO OTHERS. I WILL BLESS THOSE WHO BLESS YOU, AND I WILL CURSE THOSE WHO CURSE YOU!

OH, ABRAHAM, I KNOW WHAT GOD SAID — BUT WE'RE GETTING OLDER, AND HAVE NO CHILDREN.

IS THIS HOW GOD REWARDS YOUR LIFE OF OBEDIENCE?

SARAI, GOD HAS SPOKEN, AND ALL WE CAN DO IS WAIT AND TRUST.

AND HE SAID, I WILL CERTAINLY RETURN UNTO THEE ACCORDING TO THE TIME OF LIFE, AND, LO, SARAH THY WIFE SHALL HAVE A SON. AND SARAH HEARD IT IN THE TENT DOOR, WHICH WAS BEHIND HIM.   GENESIS 18:10

AND ABRAHAM WAS AN HUNDRED YEARS OLD, WHEN HIS SON ISAAC WAS BORN UNTO HIM. AND SARAH SAID, GOD HATH MADE ME TO LAUGH, SO THAT ALL THAT HEAR WILL LAUGH WITH ME.   GENESIS 21: 5, 6

The Story of Abraham - Genesis 11 through 22

. . . AND ABRAHAM BUILT AN ALTAR THERE, AND LAID THE WOOD IN ORDER, AND BOUND ISAAC HIS SON, AND LAID HIM ON THE ALTAR UPON THE WOOD.   GENESIS 22:9

THE STORY OF JACOB AND ESAU

... THE ONE PEOPLE SHALL BE STRONGER THAN THE OTHER PEOPLE; AND THE ELDER SHALL SERVE THE YOUNGER.   GENESIS 25:23

ISAAC AND REBEKAH HAD TWO SONS. ESAU WAS THE FIRSTBORN BY A FEW SECONDS, BUT JACOB CAME INTO THE WORLD GRIPPING HIS ANKLE; THEIR TWO LIVES CONTINUED THIS THEME.

JACOB LIVES UP TO HIS NAME — "THE DECEIVER." HE'S ALWAYS FOOLING HIS BROTHER.

WELL — GO EASY ON HIM — YOU KNOW HE'S MY FAVORITE.

YOU LIKE ESAU BEST BECAUSE HE HUNTS AND STAYS IN THE FIELDS!

IT'S NOT FAIR THAT ESAU SHOULD RULE THE TRIBE JUST BECAUSE HE'S A FEW SECONDS OLDER. I'M SMARTER AND I'LL PROVE IT —

BY GETTING THAT BIRTHRIGHT FROM HIM!

AND JACOB SOD [COOKED] POTTAGE: AND ESAU CAME
FROM THE FIELD, AND HE WAS FAINT.
GENESIS 25:29

AND JACOB SAID UNTO HIS FATHER, I AM ESAU THY FIRSTBORN; I HAVE DONE ACCORDING AS THOU BADEST ME: ARISE, I PRAY THEE, SIT AND EAT OF MY VENISON, THAT THY SOUL MAY BLESS ME.   GENESIS 27:19

AND HE DREAMED, AND BEHOLD A LADDER SET UP ON THE EARTH, AND THE TOP OF IT REACHED TO HEAVEN: AND BEHOLD THE ANGELS OF GOD ASCENDING AND DESCENDING ON IT.   GENESIS 28:12

THE STORY OF JOSEPH

NOW ISRAEL [JACOB] LOVED JOSEPH MORE THAN ALL HIS CHILDREN, BECAUSE HE WAS THE SON OF HIS OLD AGE: AND HE MADE HIM A COAT OF MANY COLOURS.   GENESIS 37:3

AND HIS BRETHREN SAID TO HIM, SHALT THOU INDEED REIGN OVER
OR SHALT THOU INDEED HAVE DOMINION OVER US? AND THEY HATED HIM
YET THE MORE FOR HIS DREAMS, AND FOR HIS WORDS.   GENESIS 37:8

COME, AND LET US SELL HIM TO THE ISHMEELITES, AND LET NOT OUR HAND BE UPON HIM; FOR HE IS OUR BROTHER AND OUR FLESH. AND HIS BRETHREN WERE CONTENT.   GENESIS 37:27

The Story of Joseph - Genesis 37 through 39

AND JOSEPH'S MASTER TOOK HIM, AND PUT HIM INTO THE PRISON, A PLACE WHERE THE KING'S PRISONERS WERE BOUND: AND HE WAS THERE IN THE PRISON.   GENESIS 39:20

WHAT COUNTRY IS THIS?

EGYPT. YOU ARE A SLAVE TO POTIPHAR, CAPTAIN OF THE KING'S GUARDS.

THAT NEW BOY IS NICE LOOKING FOR A SLAVE!

I SHOULDN'T BE ALONE WITH YOU — I AM ONLY ONE OF YOUR HUSBAND'S SLAVES!

I JUST WANT TO TALK WITH YOU! TAKE A BREAK AND HAVE SOME FUN FOR ONCE!

YOUR SLAVE ATTACKED ME — SEE, HERE'S HIS ROBE!

I'LL THROW HIM IN THE DUNGEON FOR THIS!

TWICE I'VE BEEN BETRAYED!

HOME SEEMS A MILLION MILES AWAY.

BUT GOD HAD WONDERFUL PLANS FOR JOSEPH.

The Story of Joseph - Genesis 37 through 39

29

JOSEPH IN EGYPT

... WE HAVE DREAMED A DREAM, AND THERE IS NO INTERPRETER OF IT.
AND JOSEPH SAID UNTO THEM, DO NOT INTERPRETATIONS BELONG TO
GOD? TELL ME THEM, I PRAY YOU.

GENESIS 40:8

Joseph in Egypt - Genesis 40 through 45

AND JOSEPH WAS THE GOVERNOR OVER THE LAND . . . AND JOSEPH'S BRETHREN CAME, AND BOWED DOWN THEMSELVES BEFORE HIM WITH THEIR FACES TO THE EARTH.   GENESIS 42:6

I'VE FOUND THAT MAN. JOSEPH, YOUR GOD WILL HELP YOU — AND EGYPT.

THE FAMINE COMES; AND THE WORLD COMES TO EGYPT.

THOSE TEN MEN APPROACHING — THEY LOOK FAMILIAR

YES, THEY'RE MY BROTHERS, ALL THE WAY FROM CANAAN — AND THEY DON'T RECOGNIZE ME!

YOU MEN ARE SPIES, AREN'T YOU?

OH, NO SIR! WE ARE 10 BROTHERS. WE HAVE ANOTHER AT HOME — BENJAMIN — AND ONE WHO IS DEAD.

SORRY. I DON'T BELIEVE YOU. I'M IMPRISONING ALL OF YOU.

WE'LL SEE IF THEY'VE LEARNED TO BE KIND.

BUT...

PLEASE.

WHAT WILL FATHER THINK HAS HAPPENED TO US?

WHY DOES HE ASK SO MANY QUESTIONS ABOUT OUR FAMILY?

Joseph in Egypt - Genesis 40 through 45

THEN JOSEPH COMMANDED TO FILL THEIR SACKS WITH CORN, AND TO
RESTORE EVERY MAN'S MONEY INTO HIS SACK, AND TO GIVE THEM
PROVISION FOR THE WAY.... GENESIS 42:25

Joseph in Egypt - Genesis 40 through 45

AND JOSEPH SAID UNTO HIS BRETHREN, COME NEAR TO ME, I PRAY YOU. AND THEY CAME NEAR. AND HE SAID, I AM JOSEPH YOUR BROTHER, WHOM YE SOLD INTO EGYPT.   GENESIS 45:4

THE STORY OF MOSES

AND WHEN SHE COULD NOT LONGER HIDE HIM, SHE TOOK FOR HIM AN
ARK OF BULRUSHES, AND DAUBED IT WITH SLIME AND WITH PITCH,
AND PUT THE CHILD THEREIN; AND SHE LAID IT IN THE FLAGS
BY THE RIVER'S BRINK.   EXODUS 2:3

STILL TOO MANY JEWS! I'LL HAVE ALL THEIR BABIES THROWN INTO THE RIVER!

JACOB'S SONS HAD CHILDREN, AND GRANDCHILDREN. YEARS LATER THERE WERE THOUSANDS OF HEBREWS IN EGYPT — BUT THEY BECAME SLAVES.

ONE FAMILY PLOTS TO SAVE THEIR BABY SON.

MY BASKET IS FINISHED. COME WITH ME TO THE RIVER, MIRIAM.

HE'LL BE SAFE FROM PHARAOH HERE. MIRIAM, YOU'LL STAY HIDDEN AND WATCH.

THE EGYPTIAN PRINCESS SEES THE BABY.

LOOK! A BABY IN A BASKET.

GIRL, DO YOU KNOW OF A HEBREW NURSE TO HELP CARE FOR THIS CHILD?

YES! MY MOTHER CAN DO IT!

SO THE HEBREW BOY WAS CARED FOR BY HIS OWN FAMILY — AND RAISED IN PHARAOH'S FAMILY.

AND HE LOOKED THIS WAY AND THAT WAY, AND WHEN HE SAW THAT
THERE WAS NO MAN, HE SLEW THE EGYPTIAN, AND HID HIM IN THE SAND.
EXODUS 2:12

COME NOW THEREFORE, AND I WILL SEND THEE UNTO PHARAOH,
THAT THOU MAYEST BRING FORTH MY PEOPLE THE CHILDREN OF ISRAEL
OUT OF EGYPT.   EXODUS 3:10

AND I WILL STRETCH OUT MY HAND, AND SMITE EGYPT WITH
ALL MY WONDERS WHICH I WILL DO IN THE MIDST THEREOF:
AND AFTER THAT HE WILL LET YOU GO.   EXODUS 3:20

MOSES AND THE EXODUS

AND THE CHILDREN OF ISRAEL JOURNEYED ... ABOUT SIX HUNDRED
THOUSAND ON FOOT THAT WERE MEN, BESIDE CHILDREN ... AND
FLOCKS, AND HERDS, EVEN VERY MUCH CATTLE.   EXODUS 12:37-38

Moses and the Exodus - Exodus 12 through 25

BUT LIFT THOU UP THY ROD, AND STRETCH OUT THINE HAND OVER THE SEA, AND DIVIDE IT: AND THE CHILDREN OF ISRAEL SHALL GO ON DRY GROUND THROUGH THE MIDST OF THE SEA.   EXODUS 14:16

AND THE LORD CAME DOWN UPON MOUNT SINAI, ON THE TOP OF THE
MOUNT: AND THE LORD CALLED MOSES UP TO THE TOP OF THE MOUNT;
AND MOSES WENT UP.   EXODUS 19:20

Moses and the Exodus - Exodus 12 through 25

AND LET THEM MAKE ME A SANCTUARY; THAT I MAY DWELL AMONG THEM. ACCORDING TO ALL THAT I SHEW THEE, AFTER THE PATTERN OF THE TABERNACLE, AND THE PATTERN OF ALL THE INSTRUMENTS THEREOF, EVEN SO SHALL YE MAKE IT. EXODUS 25:8-9

THE CALF IS DESTROYED. DO YOU THINK MOSES WILL FORGIVE US?

THE QUESTION IS — WILL GOD? MOSES HAS GONE BACK TO THE MOUNTAIN TO PLEAD FOR US.

HERE HE COMES — AND HIS FACE IS BRIGHT AS SUNLIGHT!

GOD FORGIVES — AND HE HAS A WONDERFUL NEW PLAN!

"WE ARE TO BUILD A HOUSE OF GOD — A TABERNACLE. IT WILL BE A PLACE FOR THE SACRED ARK HOLDING THE TABLETS I BROUGHT DOWN FROM SINAI."

FROM THEN ON, THE ARK IS CARRIED IN FRONT. THEY FOLLOW GOD'S CLOUD TO THE PROMISED LAND.

JOSHUA AND CALEB

FOR I KNOW THY REBELLION, AND THY STIFF NECK: BEHOLD, WHILE I AM YET ALIVE WITH YOU THIS DAY, YE HAVE BEEN REBELLIOUS AGAINST THE LORD . . . . DEUTERONOMY 31:27

Joshua and Caleb - Numbers 13 and 14

SEND THOU MEN, THAT THEY MAY SEARCH THE LAND OF CANAAN, WHICH I GIVE UNTO THE CHILDREN OF ISRAEL: OF EVERY TRIBE OF THEIR FATHERS SHALL YE SEND A MAN .... NUMBERS 13:2

MOSES TAKES HIS RIGHT-HAND MAN ASIDE.

JOSHUA, AFTER ALL THESE YEARS WE'RE AT THE BORDER OF THE PROMISED LAND — CANAAN.

I'M CALLING FOR A MAN FROM EACH OF THE 12 TRIBES TO PLAN OUR STRATEGY — INCLUDING YOU AND CALEB.

MEN, YOU WILL MAKE A DANGEROUS JOURNEY TO SCOUT OUT THE LAND.

FIND OUT ABOUT THE LAND AND THE ARMIES.

SO, THE 12 SPIES BEGIN THEIR JOURNEY.

Joshua and Caleb - Numbers 13 and 14

AND THERE WE SAW THE GIANTS, THE SONS OF ANAK, WHICH COME OF THE GIANTS: AND WE WERE IN OUR OWN SIGHT AS GRASSHOPPERS, AND SO WE WERE IN THEIR SIGHT.   NUMBERS 13:33

Joshua and Caleb - Numbers 13 and 14

SURELY THEY SHALL NOT SEE THE LAND WHICH I SWARE UNTO THEIR FATHERS, NEITHER SHALL ANY OF THEM THAT PROVOKED ME SEE IT.
NUMBERS 14:23

JOSHUA AT JERICHO

AND JOSHUA THE SON OF NUN SENT OUT OF SHITTIM TWO MEN TO SPY
SECRETLY, SAYING, GO VIEW THE LAND, EVEN JERICHO . . . .
JOSHUA 2:1

BEHOLD, WHEN WE COME INTO THE LAND, THOU SHALT BIND THIS LINE OF SCARLET THREAD IN THE WINDOW WHICH THOU DIDST LET US DOWN BY .... JOSHUA 2:18

AND THE PRIESTS THAT BARE THE ARK OF THE COVENANT OF THE LORD STOOD FIRM ON DRY GROUND IN THE MIDST OF JORDAN, AND ALL THE ISRAELITES PASSED OVER ON DRY GROUND . . . .   JOSHUA 3:17

Joshua at Jericho - Joshua 2 through 6

AND YE SHALL COMPASS THE CITY, ALL YE MEN OF WAR, AND GO ROUND
ABOUT THE CITY ONCE. THUS SHALT THOU DO SIX DAYS.
JOSHUA 6:3

DEBORAH THE JUDGE

AND THE LORD SOLD THEM INTO THE HAND OF JABIN KING OF CANAAN,
THAT REIGNED IN HAZOR; THE CAPTAIN OF WHOSE HOST
WAS SISERA . . . .   JUDGES 4:2

AFTER THE TIME OF MOSES AND JOSHUA, THE ISRAELITES SETTLED IN CANAAN. THEY NO LONGER NEEDED GOD'S CLOUD TO GUIDE THEM THROUGH THE DESERT, OR HIS MANNA FOR FOOD, AND THEY BEGAN TO FORGET THE TRUE GOD.

THE MORE THEY FORGOT GOD, THE WEAKER THEY BECAME — AND OTHER TRIBES RAIDED THEM.

Deborah the Judge - Judges 4 and 5

AND SHE DWELT UNDER THE PALM TREE OF DEBORAH BETWEEN RAMAH AND BETH-EL IN MOUNT EPHRAIM: AND THE CHILDREN OF ISRAEL CAME UP TO HER FOR JUDGMENT. JUDGES 4:5

GO FOR BARAK THE CAPTAIN AND TELL HIM I NEED HIM IMMEDIATELY.

HE IS IN THE NORTH LAND.

BARAK, OUR JUDGE DEBORAH NEEDS YOU TO APPEAR BEFORE HER. COME WITH ME!

BARAK, TAKE 10,000 MEN TO MOUNT TABOR. JABIN'S MAN, SISERA, WILL COME WITH HIS TROOPS TO DESTROY YOU. BUT HE WON'T BE COUNTING ON THE POWER OF GOD!

I'LL DO IT IMMEDIATELY... BUT WILL YOU COME, TOO? GOD SPEAKS THROUGH YOU!

YES, I WILL. BUT THIS SHOWS YOU LACK FAITH OF YOUR OWN, SO YOU WILL NOT PERSONALLY HAVE THIS VICTORY. A WOMAN WILL PUT SISERA AWAY INSTEAD.

Deborah the Judge - Judges 4 and 5

AND DEBORAH SAID UNTO BARAK, UP; FOR THIS IS THE DAY IN WHICH THE LORD HATH DELIVERED SISERA INTO THINE HAND: IS NOT THE LORD GONE OUT BEFORE THEE? . . . . JUDGES 4:14

DEBORAH LEADS THE ISRAELITES TO MOUNT TABOR.

JUST WAIT — THE CANAANITES WILL BE HERE SOON.

SISERA, MY SCOUTS SAY THE ISRAELITES ARE ON TABOR. TAKE ALL OUR MEN AND CRUSH THEM FOREVER.

YES, JABIN!

GO, BARAK! GOD WILL DELIVER SISERA AND ALL HIS MEN TO YOU! DON'T YOU HAVE FAITH?

...AND ALL THE HOST OF SISERA FELL UPON THE EDGE OF THE SWORD; AND THERE WAS NOT A MAN LEFT. HOWBEIT SISERA FLED AWAY ON HIS FEET TO THE TENT .... JUDGES 4:16-17

THE STORY OF GIDEON

... AND HIS SON GIDEON THRESHED WHEAT BY THE WINEPRESS, TO HIDE IT FROM THE MIDIANITES. AND THE ANGEL OF THE LORD APPEARED UNTO HIM, AND SAID UNTO HIM, THE LORD IS WITH THEE, THOU MIGHTY MAN OF VALOUR.   JUDGES 6:11-12

AND GIDEON SAID UNTO GOD, IF THOU WILT SAVE ISRAEL BY MINE HAND, AS THOU HAST SAID, BEHOLD, I WILL PUT A FLEECE OF WOOL IN THE FLOOR . . . .   JUDGES 6:36-37

NOW THEREFORE GO TO, PROCLAIM IN THE EARS OF THE PEOPLE, SAYING, WHOSOEVER IS FEARFUL AND AFRAID, LET HIM RETURN AND DEPART EARLY FROM MOUNT GILEAD.   JUDGES 7:3

The Story of Gideon - Judges 6 and 7

... BEHOLD, I DREAMED A DREAM, AND, LO, A CAKE OF BARLEY BREAD TUMBLED INTO THE HOST OF MIDIAN, AND CAME UNTO A TENT, AND SMOTE IT THAT IT FELL, AND OVERTURNED IT, THAT THE TENT LAY ALONG.

JUDGES 7:13

THAT NIGHT...

THE LORD SPOKE TO ME IN A DREAM. WE'RE VASTLY OUTNUMBERED, BUT HE WILL LEAD US TO VICTORY!

I HAD THAT DREAM, TOO — IT'S TIME TO GET THE MEN IN PLACE AND BLOW THE TRUMPET.

BLOWING THEIR TRUMPETS AND SMASHING THE JARS IN THE MIDDLE OF THE NIGHT, 300 MEN SOUND LIKE 30,000 THUNDERING DOWN UPON THE MIDIANITES.

THE SWORD OF THE LORD, AND OF GIDEON!

OUR MEN ARE PANICKING! THEY'RE FLEEING THE ISRAELITES, AND EVEN ATTACKING EACH OTHER!

THESE ISRAELITES — WHAT IS THEIR SECRET?

WHAT ARE NUMBERS TO THE LORD? HE'S ONLY LOOKING FOR A FEW GOOD MEN!

The Story of Gideon - Judges 6 and 7

THE STORY OF SAMSON

AND THE WOMAN BARE A SON, AND CALLED HIS NAME SAMSON: AND
THE CHILD GREW, AND THE LORD BLESSED HIM.

JUDGES 13:24

The Story of Samson - Judges 13 through 16

AND DELILAH SAID TO SAMSON, TELL ME, I PRAY THEE, WHEREIN THY GREAT STRENGTH LIETH, AND WHEREWITH THOU MIGHTEST BE BOUND TO AFFLICT THEE.   JUDGES 16:6

... IF I BE SHAVEN, THEN MY STRENGTH WILL GO FROM ME, AND I SHALL
BECOME WEAK, AND BE LIKE ANY OTHER MAN.
JUDGES 16:17

The Story of Samson - Judges 13 through 16

... O LORD GOD, REMEMBER ME, I PRAY THEE, AND STRENGTHEN ME, I PRAY THEE, ONLY THIS ONCE, O GOD, THAT I MAY BE AT ONCE AVENGED OF THE PHILISTINES FOR MY TWO EYES.   JUDGES 16:28

IN PULLING DOWN THE TEMPLE, SAMSON KILLS MORE PHILISTINES IN DEATH THAN HE DID IN LIFE!

THE STORY OF RUTH

... FOR WHITHER THOU GOEST, I WILL GO; AND WHERE THOU LODGEST, I WILL LODGE: THY PEOPLE SHALL BE MY PEOPLE, AND THY GOD MY GOD.

RUTH 1:16

THEN SAID BOAZ UNTO RUTH, HEAREST THOU NOT, MY DAUGHTER? GO NOT TO GLEAN IN ANOTHER FIELD, NEITHER GO FROM HENCE, BUT ABIDE HERE FAST BY MY MAIDENS.   RUTH 2:8

AND NOW, MY DAUGHTER, FEAR NOT; I WILL DO TO THEE ALL THAT THOU REQUIREST: FOR ALL THE CITY OF MY PEOPLE DOTH KNOW THAT THOU ART A VIRTUOUS WOMAN.   RUTH 3:11

AND THE WOMEN HER NEIGHBOURS GAVE IT A NAME, SAYING, THERE IS A SON BORN TO NAOMI; AND THEY CALLED HIS NAME OBED: HE IS THE FATHER OF JESSE, THE FATHER OF DAVID.　　RUTH 4:17

ALL BETHLEHEM GATHERS FOR THE WEDDING OF BOAZ AND RUTH.

WHEN MY HUSBAND DIED, I THOUGHT THERE WAS NO MORE JOY IN LIFE. THANK YOU, RUTH, FOR BRINGING ME HERE.

SOON THERE IS A BABY BOY, OBED. HE WILL BE THE GRANDFATHER OF KING DAVID — AND AN ANCESTOR OF ANOTHER KING BORN IN BETHLEHEM MANY YEARS LATER.

THE STORY OF SAMUEL

AND SHE VOWED A VOW, AND SAID, O LORD OF HOSTS, IF THOU WILT
... GIVE UNTO THINE HANDMAID A MAN CHILD, THEN I WILL GIVE HIM
UNTO THE LORD ALL THE DAYS OF HIS LIFE ....   1 SAMUEL 1:11

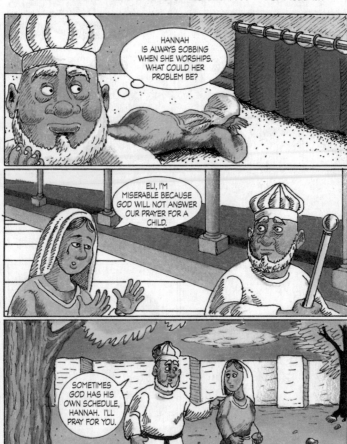

THEREFORE ALSO I HAVE LENT HIM TO THE LORD; AS LONG AS HE LIVETH HE SHALL BE LENT TO THE LORD. AND HE WORSHIPPED THE LORD THERE.   1 SAMUEL 1:28

AND THE LORD CALLED YET AGAIN, SAMUEL. AND SAMUEL AROSE AND
WENT TO ELI, AND SAID, HERE AM I; FOR THOU DIDST CALL ME. AND HE
ANSWERED, I CALLED NOT, MY SON .... 1 SAMUEL 3:6

The Story of Samuel - 1 Samuel 1 through 3

AND THE LORD SAID TO SAMUEL, BEHOLD, I WILL DO A THING IN ISRAEL, AT WHICH BOTH THE EARS OF EVERY ONE THAT HEARETH IT SHALL TINGLE.   1 SAMUEL 3:11

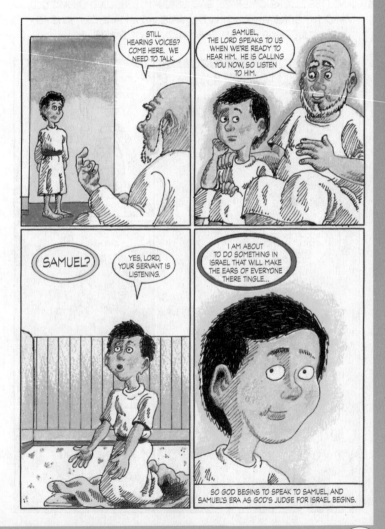

ISRAEL'S FIRST KING

AND [THE ELDERS OF ISRAEL] SAID UNTO HIM, BEHOLD, THOU ART OLD,
AND THY SONS WALK NOT IN THY WAYS: NOW MAKE US A KING TO
JUDGE US LIKE ALL THE NATIONS.   1 SAMUEL 8:5

AND WHEN SAMUEL SAW SAUL, THE LORD SAID UNTO HIM, BEHOLD THE MAN WHOM I SPAKE TO THEE OF! THIS SAME SHALL REIGN OVER MY PEOPLE.   1 SAMUEL 9:17

THEREFORE THEY ENQUIRED OF THE LORD FURTHER, IF THE MAN SHOULD YET COME THITHER. AND THE LORD ANSWERED, BEHOLD, HE HATH HID HIMSELF AMONG THE STUFF.   1 SAMUEL 10:22

Israel's First King - 1 Samuel 7 through 13

AND SAMUEL SAID TO SAUL, THOU HAST DONE FOOLISHLY: THOU HAST NOT KEPT THE COMMANDMENT OF THE LORD THY GOD, WHICH HE COMMANDED THEE . . . . 1 SAMUEL 13:13

DAVID AND GOLIATH

THEN SAMUEL TOOK THE HORN OF OIL, AND ANOINTED HIM IN THE MIDST OF HIS BRETHREN: AND THE SPIRIT OF THE LORD CAME UPON DAVID FROM THAT DAY FORWARD .... 1 SAMUEL 16:13

AND SAUL SENT TO JESSE, SAYING, LET DAVID, I PRAY THEE, STAND BEFORE ME; FOR HE HATH FOUND FAVOUR IN MY SIGHT.
1 SAMUEL 16:22

David and Goliath - 1 Samuel 16 and 17

AND DAVID ROSE UP EARLY IN THE MORNING, AND LEFT THE SHEEP WITH A KEEPER, . . . AND HE CAME TO THE TRENCH, AS THE HOST WAS GOING FORTH TO THE FIGHT, AND SHOUTED FOR THE BATTLE.
1 SAMUEL 17:20

David and Goliath - 1 Samuel 16 and 17

AND DAVID PUT HIS HAND IN HIS BAG, AND TOOK THENCE A STONE, AND
SLANG IT, AND SMOTE THE PHILISTINE IN HIS FOREHEAD; AND HE FELL
UPON HIS FACE TO THE EARTH.
1 SAMUEL 17:49

DAVID BECOMES AN INSTANT
HERO, AND THE PHILISTINES'
POWER OVER ISRAEL IS BROKEN.

DAVID THE KING

AND DAVID PERCEIVED THAT THE LORD HAD ESTABLISHED HIM KING OVER ISRAEL, AND THAT HE HAD EXALTED HIS KINGDOM FOR HIS PEOPLE ISRAEL'S SAKE.   2 SAMUEL 5:12

DAVID BECOMES KING AFTER SAUL'S DEATH.

HAIL TO THE NEW KING!

KING SAUL WANDERED FROM GOD, BUT DAVID WILL BRING US GOD'S FAVOR, ONCE AGAIN.

UNDER HIS LEADERSHIP, ISRAEL IS POWERFUL.

WE USED TO HUMILIATE THE ISRAELITES. NOW THE TABLES ARE TURNED.

NATHAN, YOU ARE GOD'S PROPHET. DON'T YOU THINK WE SHOULD HONOR GOD IN JERUSALEM BY BRINGING BACK THE ARK OF THE COVENANT?

YES! PUT IT WHERE THE PEOPLE CAN SEE IT!

AND DAVID AROSE, AND WENT WITH ALL THE PEOPLE THAT WERE WITH HIM FROM BAALE OF JUDAH, TO BRING UP FROM THENCE THE ARK OF GOD .... 2 SAMUEL 6:2

THE ARK HOLDING THE 10 COMMANDMENTS HAD BEEN NEARLY FORGOTTEN. NOW, DAVID BRINGS IT INTO JERUSALEM WITH MUSIC AND CELEBRATION!

LORD, THE HOLY ARK IS DISPLAYED IN A TATTERED TENT. I WOULD LIKE TO BUILD A HOUSE THAT IS WORTHY FOR YOU TO DWELL IN.

NATHAN, GOD HAS SPOKEN TO ME. THE TEMPLE WILL BE BUILT — BUT BY ONE TO COME AFTER ME.

GOD HAS HIS OWN TIMES AND SEASONS.

ALONG WITH THE TRADITION OF THE TIME, DAVID TAKES MANY WIVES.

... AND FROM THE ROOF HE SAW A WOMAN WASHING HERSELF; AND THE WOMAN WAS VERY BEAUTIFUL TO LOOK UPON. AND DAVID SENT AND INQUIRED AFTER THE WOMAN .... 2 SAMUEL 11:2-3

David the King - 2 Samuel 5 through 12

AND DAVID SAID UNTO NATHAN, I HAVE SINNED AGAINST THE LORD. AND
NATHAN SAID UNTO DAVID, THE LORD ALSO HATH PUT AWAY THY SIN;
THOU SHALT NOT DIE.   2 SAMUEL 12:13

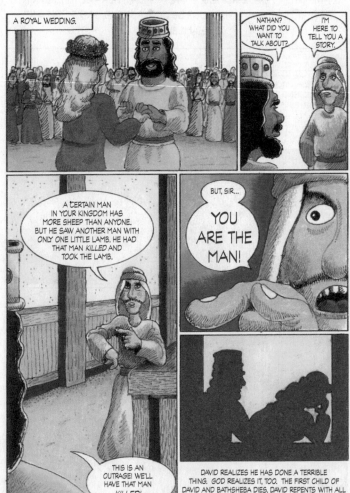

DAVID AND ABSALOM

...AND WHEN I SAY UNTO YOU, SMITE AMNON; THEN KILL HIM, FEAR NOT: HAVE NOT I COMMANDED YOU? BE COURAGEOUS, AND BE VALIANT.

2 SAMUEL 13:28

DAVID WORKS TO MAKE ISRAEL ONE OF THE WORLD'S GREAT NATIONS, BUT THERE ARE PROBLEMS IN HIS FAMILY.

ABSALOM, I KNOW AMNON DID SOMETHING TERRIBLE — A WICKED THING. BUT YOU MUST FORGIVE HIM. YOU ARE BOTH MY SONS.

OF COURSE, FATHER. I'M HAVING A FEAST AND AMNON IS INVITED.

AMNON IS INVITED ALL RIGHT — AND WHEN I GIVE THE SIGNAL, YOUR MEN WILL KILL HIM!

WHAT IS GOING ON?

AMNON HURT AND HUMILIATED ABSALOM'S SISTER — HIS OWN HALF-SISTER. ABSALOM SWORE REVENGE.

SO ABSALOM FLED, AND WENT TO GESHUR, AND WAS THERE THREE YEARS. AND THE SOUL OF KING DAVID LONGED TO GO FORTH UNTO ABSALOM . . . . 2 SAMUEL 13:38-39

... AND WHEN HE HAD CALLED FOR ABSALOM, HE CAME TO THE KING,
AND BOWED HIMSELF ON HIS FACE TO THE GROUND BEFORE THE KING:
AND THE KING KISSED ABSALOM.   2 SAMUEL 14:33

David and Absalom - 2 Samuel 13 through 18

. . . AND HIS HEAD CAUGHT HOLD OF THE OAK, AND HE WAS TAKEN UP BETWEEN THE HEAVEN AND THE EARTH; AND THE MULE THAT WAS UNDER HIM WENT AWAY.   2 SAMUEL 18:9

MEN, I BELIEVE THE TIME IS RIGHT. WE HAVE ENOUGH SOLDIERS TO TAKE THE KINGDOM. INVITE ALL THE TRIBES TO HEBRON. WE'LL UNITE THERE AND OVERTHROW MY FATHER!

KING DAVID! YOUR SON IS GATHERING TROOPS AT HEBRON — YOUR LIFE IS IN DANGER!

MY OWN SON! YES, I EXPECTED IT.

I MUST PROTECT MY FAMILY AND LOYAL FRIENDS. WE'LL LEAVE JERUSALEM!

THE BATTLE COMES TO THE FOREST OF EPHRAIM. DAVID'S ARMY OVERWHELMS ABSALOM'S.

AS HE FLEES IN PANIC, ABSALOM'S HAIR IS CAUGHT IN A LOW BRANCH. JOAB'S SOLDIERS KILL HIM THERE.

AGAIN, MY HEART IS BROKEN. I CAN LEAD A *NATION*, BUT *NOT* MY OWN FAMILY.

YET THE BEST DAYS ARE STILL TO COME FOR ISRAEL, AND *ANOTHER* SON OF DAVID.

David and Absalom - 2 Samuel 13 through 18

ISRAEL'S WISEST KING

THEN SAT SOLOMON UPON THE THRONE OF DAVID HIS FATHER; AND HIS
KINGDOM WAS ESTABLISHED GREATLY.   1 KINGS 2:12

...AND HE CAME TO JERUSALEM, AND STOOD BEFORE THE ARK OF THE COVENANT OF THE LORD, AND OFFERED UP BURNT-OFFERINGS, AND OFFERED PEACE-OFFERINGS, AND MADE A FEAST TO ALL HIS SERVANTS.
1 KINGS 3:15

THEN CAME THERE TWO WOMEN, THAT WERE HARLOTS, UNTO THE KING, AND STOOD BEFORE HIM.   1 KINGS 3:16

Israel's Wisest King - 1 Kings 2 and 3

AND ALL ISRAEL HEARD OF THE JUDGMENT WHICH THE KING HAD JUDGED; AND THEY FEARED THE KING: FOR THEY SAW THAT THE WISDOM OF GOD WAS IN HIM, TO DO JUDGMENT.   1 KINGS 3:28

SOLOMON'S TEMPLE

AND, BEHOLD, I PURPOSE TO BUILD AN HOUSE UNTO THE NAME OF THE
LORD MY GOD, AS THE LORD SPAKE UNTO DAVID MY FATHER . . . .
1 KINGS 5:5

AND HE BUILT THE WALLS OF THE HOUSE WITHIN WITH BOARDS OF CEDAR, BOTH THE FLOOR OF THE HOUSE, AND THE WALLS OF THE CEILING: AND HE COVERED THEM ON THE INSIDE WITH WOOD ....

1 KINGS 6:15

...SO WE TIE THE LOGS TOGETHER LIKE RAFTS AND FLOAT THEM TO ISRAEL FOR THE TEMPLE!

BEAUTIFUL MARBLE IS BROUGHT OUT OF QUARRIES.

SON, YOU AND YOUR OWN CHILDREN WILL PASS THROUGH THESE GOLDEN DOORS — AND MANY GENERATIONS TO COME.

Solomon's Temple - 1 Kings 5 through 11

AND IN THE ELEVENTH YEAR, . . .WAS THE HOUSE FINISHED THROUGH-
OUT ALL THE PARTS THEREOF, AND ACCORDING TO ALL THE FASHION OF
IT. SO WAS HE SEVEN YEARS IN BUILDING IT.

1 KINGS 6:38

AND AHIJAH CAUGHT THE NEW GARMENT THAT WAS ON HIM, AND RENT IT IN TWELVE PIECES: . . . FOR THUS SAITH THE LORD, THE GOD OF ISRAEL, BEHOLD, I WILL REND THE KINGDOM OUT OF THE HAND OF SOLOMON, AND WILL GIVE TEN TRIBES TO THEE.   1 KINGS 11:30-31

Solomon's Temple - 1 Kings 5 through 11

FIRE ON THE MOUNTAIN

SO THEY DIVIDED THE LAND BETWEEN THEM TO PASS THROUGHOUT IT: AHAB WENT ONE WAY BY HIMSELF, AND OBADIAH WENT ANOTHER WAY BY HIMSELF.   1 KINGS 18:6

SOLOMON HAS ALLOWED THE PEOPLE TO WORSHIP FALSE GODS, AND THE LORD IS *NOT* PLEASED.

YOU HAVE DISOBEYED ME, SO YOUR KINGDOM SHALL FALL. BUT BECAUSE OF MY LOVE FOR DAVID, YOUR FATHER, IT WILL NOT HAPPEN DURING YOUR LIFETIME.

THE SPLIT COMES AFTER SOLOMON DIES. THE NORTHERN TRIBES ARE STILL CALLED ISRAEL, WHILE THE SOUTHERN TRIBES ARE CALLED JUDAH.

GREAT SEA

ISRAEL

SALT SEA

JUDAH

ISRAEL'S KING AHAB MARRIES A PRINCESS FROM TYRE, WHERE FALSE GODS WERE WORSHIPED.

MEET JEZEBEL, YOUR QUEEN. YOU WILL OBEY HER AS YOU DO ME!

SO AHAB SENT UNTO ALL THE CHILDREN OF ISRAEL, AND GATHERED THE PROPHETS TOGETHER UNTO MOUNT CARMEL.   1 KINGS 18:20

Fire on the Mountain - 1 Kings 18

HEAR ME, O LORD, HEAR ME, THAT THIS PEOPLE MAY KNOW THAT THOU ART THE LORD GOD, AND THAT THOU HAST TURNED THEIR HEART BACK AGAIN.   1 KINGS 18:37

Fire on the Mountain - 1 Kings 18

A CHARIOT OF FIRE

AND WHEN HE SAW THAT, HE AROSE, AND WENT FOR HIS LIFE, AND CAME TO BEER-SHEBA, WHICH BELONGETH TO JUDAH, AND LEFT HIS SERVANT THERE. BUT HE HIMSELF WENT A DAY'S JOURNEY INTO THE WILDERNESS .... 1 KINGS 19:3-4

Chariot of Fire - 1 Kings 19 and 2 Kings 2

...FOR THE CHILDREN OF ISRAEL HAVE FORSAKEN THY COVENANT, THROWN DOWN THINE ALTARS, AND SLAIN THY PROPHETS WITH THE SWORD; AND I, EVEN I ONLY, AM LEFT .... 1 KINGS 19:10

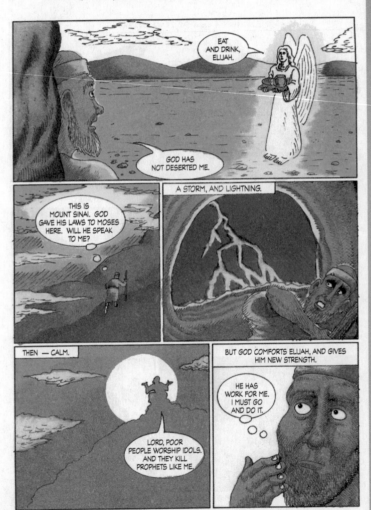

AND ELIJAH TOOK HIS MANTLE, AND WRAPPED IT TOGETHER, AND SMOTE
THE WATERS, AND THEY WERE DIVIDED HITHER AND THITHER, SO THAT
THEY TWO WENT OVER ON DRY GROUND.   2 KINGS 2:8

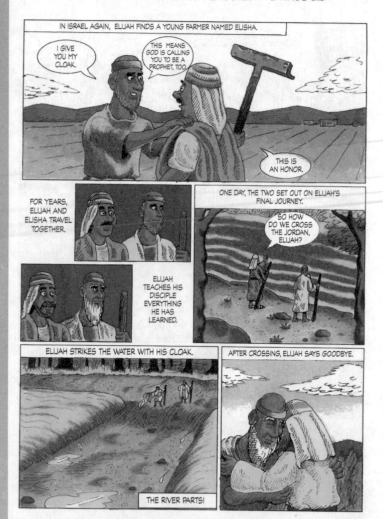

Chariot of Fire - 1 Kings 19 and 2 Kings 2

.... BEHOLD, THERE APPEARED A CHARIOT OF FIRE, AND HORSES OF FIRE, AND PARTED THEM BOTH ASUNDER; AND ELIJAH WENT UP BY A WHIRLWIND INTO HEAVEN.   2 KINGS 2:11

IN A MIGHTY WHIRLWIND, A CHARIOT OF FIRE TAKES ELIJAH INTO THE HEAVENS.

ELIJAH IS ON HIS WAY HOME.

Chariot of Fire - 1 Kings 19 and 2 Kings 2

ELISHA THE PROPHET

NOW THERE CRIED A CERTAIN WOMAN OF THE WIVES OF THE SONS OF THE PROPHETS UNTO ELISHA, SAYING, THY SERVANT MY HUSBAND IS DEAD ... AND THE CREDITOR IS COME TO TAKE UNTO HIM MY TWO SONS TO BE BONDMEN.   2 KINGS 4:1

THEN HE SAID, GO, BORROW THEE VESSELS ABROAD OF ALL THY NEIGHBOURS, EVEN EMPTY VESSELS; BORROW NOT A FEW.
2 KINGS 4:3

FOR THE LORD HAD MADE THE HOST OF THE SYRIANS TO HEAR A NOISE
OF CHARIOTS, AND A NOISE OF HORSES, EVEN THE NOISE
OF A GREAT HOST . . . .   2 KINGS 7:6

ISRAEL IS AT WAR WITH SYRIA, AND...

WE SET TRAPS FOR ISRAEL, BUT ELISHA SEEMS TO KNOW OUR EVERY MOVE... HE WARNS THEM EVERY TIME!

OUR SPIES SAY HE IS IN DOTHAN. SEND THE ARMY THERE AND KILL HIM!

ELISHA, IT'S THE ENTIRE SYRIAN ARMY.

DON'T WORRY, GOD'S BIGGER THAN ANY ARMY.

ELISHA COMES OUT TO MEET THEM...BUT THEY SEE A VISION OF FIERY CHARIOTS AROUND HIM.

Elisha the Prophet - 2 Kings 4 through 6

... ELISHA PRAYED UNTO THE LORD, AND SAID, SMITE THIS PEOPLE, I PRAY THEE, WITH BLINDNESS. AND HE SMOTE THEM WITH BLINDNESS ACCORDING TO THE WORD OF ELISHA.   2 KINGS 6:18

THE STORY OF KING JOSIAH

JOSIAH WAS EIGHT YEARS OLD WHEN HE BEGAN TO REIGN, . . . AND HE DID THAT WHICH WAS RIGHT IN THE SIGHT OF THE LORD, AND WALKED IN ALL THE WAY OF DAVID HIS FATHER . . . . 2 KINGS 22:1-2

The Story of King Josiah - 2 Kings 22

...AND LET THEM GIVE IT TO THE DOERS OF THE WORK WHICH IS IN THE HOUSE OF THE LORD, TO REPAIR THE BREACHES OF THE HOUSE, UNTO CARPENTERS, AND BUILDERS, AND MASONS, AND TO BUY TIMBER AND HEWN STONE TO REPAIR THE HOUSE.   2 KINGS 22:5-6

AND SHAPHAN THE SCRIBE SHEWED THE KING, SAYING, HILKIAH THE PRIEST HATH DELIVERED ME A BOOK. AND SHAPHAN READ IT BEFORE THE KING.   2 KINGS 22:10

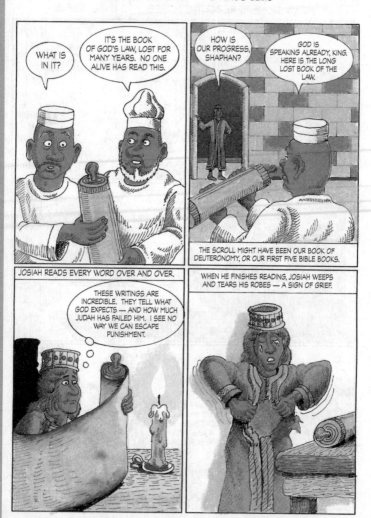

AND THE KING STOOD BY A PILLAR, AND MADE A COVENANT BEFORE THE
LORD, TO WALK AFTER THE LORD, AND TO KEEP HIS COMMANDMENTS
AND HIS TESTIMONIES AND HIS STATUTES WITH ALL THEIR HEART AND
ALL THEIR SOUL . . . .   2 KINGS 23:3

The Story of King Josiah - 2 Kings 22

EZRA: THE HOMECOMING

AND THEM THAT HAD ESCAPED FROM THE SWORD CARRIED HE AWAY TO
BABYLON; WHERE THEY WERE SERVANTS TO HIM AND HIS SONS UNTIL
THE REIGN OF THE KINGDOM OF PERSIA.   2 CHRONICLES 36:20

JOSIAH PROVES TO BE THE LAST GREAT KING OF JUDAH. AFTER HIS TIME, THE COUNTRY
TURNS BACK TO IDOLS AND BECOMES WEAKER. IN 586 B.C., THE POWERFUL BABYLONIAN
ARMY DESTROYS JERUSALEM AND CARRIES AWAY THE JEWS TO BABYLON.

FOR MANY YEARS THE JEWS ARE AWAY FROM THEIR TRUE HOME.

JERUSALEM WAS BEAUTIFUL. WE HAD A WONDERFUL TEMPLE FOR GOD.

MAYBE SOMEDAY I'LL GO THERE!

NEVER! GOD HAS FORGOTTEN US.

NO, THERE'S HOPE — BABYLON HAS FALLEN TO PERSIA, AND THEY SAY KING CYRUS WILL BE GOOD TO THE JEWS.

THUS SAITH CYRUS KING OF PERSIA, THE LORD GOD OF HEAVEN HATH
GIVEN ME ALL THE KINGDOMS OF THE EARTH; AND HE HATH CHARGED
ME TO BUILD HIM AN HOUSE AT JERUSALEM, WHICH IS IN JUDAH.
EZRA 1:2

AND WHEN THE SEVENTH MONTH WAS COME, AND THE CHILDREN OF ISRAEL WERE IN THE CITIES, THE PEOPLE GATHERED THEMSELVES TOGETHER AS ONE MAN TO JERUSALEM.   EZRA 3:1

JERUSALEM IS UP AHEAD. AFTER ALL THESE YEARS, WHAT WILL IT LOOK LIKE?

THEIR HEARTS SINK AS THEY SEE THE RUINS.

DON'T BE DISCOURAGED! WE MUST BUILD AGAIN. IT'S IN BAD REPAIR, BUT IT'S HOME. WE SHOULD EACH MAKE AN OFFERING FOR THE REBUILDING OF THE TEMPLE.

FOR NOW, IT'S JUST AN ALTAR. BUT AROUND IT, WHERE THE TEMPLE ONCE STOOD, IT WILL RISE AGAIN!

BUT TROUBLE COMES FROM THE SAMARITANS, WHO LIVE NEARBY.

THE JEWS DON'T WANT US NEAR THEIR TEMPLE BECAUSE WE WORSHIP OTHER GODS.

WE'LL SEE THAT NO TEMPLE IS BUILT AT ALL. WE'LL WRITE THE NEW PERSIAN KING.

TO KING ARTAXERXES — YOU SHOULD KNOW THE JEWS ARE REBUILDING THE EVIL CITY OF JERUSALEM. IF THE WALLS GO UP AGAIN, THEY WILL STOP PAYING TAXES TO YOU.

— THE SAMARITANS.

BLESSED BE THE LORD GOD OF OUR FATHERS, WHICH HATH PUT SUCH A THING AS THIS IN THE KING'S HEART, TO BEAUTIFY THE HOUSE OF THE LORD WHICH IS IN JERUSALEM.   EZRA 7:27

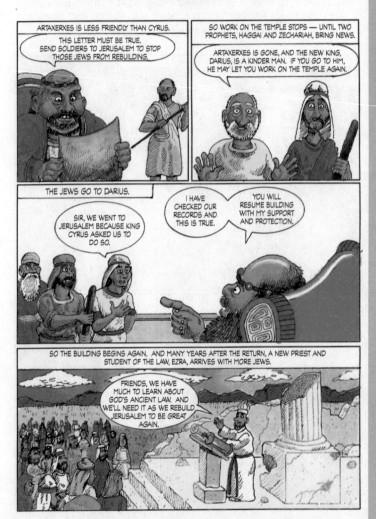

NEHEMIAH AND THE WALLS

AND IT CAME TO PASS, WHEN I HEARD THESE WORDS, THAT I SAT DOWN AND WEPT, AND MOURNED CERTAIN DAYS, AND FASTED, AND PRAYED BEFORE THE GOD OF HEAVEN.   NEHEMIAH 1:4

NEHEMIAH IS A CUPBEARER TO THE PERSIAN KING.

HELLO, FRIENDS! YOU'VE COME FROM JUDAH, MY NATIVE LAND. HOW ARE THINGS THERE?

NOT GOOD. WE HAVE NO WALLS, AND ANY PASSING TRIBE CAN RAID US.

THIS IS AWFUL NEWS. BUT WHAT CAN I DO A THOUSAND MILES AWAY, EXCEPT PRAY? OR MAYBE...

MAYBE...

AND I SAID UNTO THE KING, IF IT PLEASE THE KING, AND IF THY SERVANT
HAVE FOUND FAVOUR IN THY SIGHT, THAT THOU WOULDEST SEND ME
UNTO JUDAH .... NEHEMIAH 2:5

THEN ANSWERED I THEM, AND SAID UNTO THEM, THE GOD OF HEAVEN, HE WILL PROSPER US; THEREFORE WE HIS SERVANTS WILL ARISE AND BUILD .... NEHEMIAH 2:20

Nehemiah and the Walls - Nehemiah

SO BUILT WE THE WALL; AND ALL THE WALL WAS JOINED TOGETHER UNTO THE HALF THEREOF: FOR THE PEOPLE HAD A MIND TO WORK.
NEHEMIAH 4:6

ESTHER THE QUEEN

AND THE KING LOVED ESTHER ABOVE ALL THE WOMEN, AND SHE OBTAINED GRACE AND FAVOUR IN HIS SIGHT ... SO THAT HE SET THE ROYAL CROWN UPON HER HEAD .... ESTHER 2:17

AND ESTHER SAID, THE ADVERSARY AND ENEMY IS THIS WICKED HAMAN.
THEN HAMAN WAS AFRAID BEFORE THE KING AND THE QUEEN.
ESTHER 7:6

AND WHEN HAMAN SAW THAT MORDECAI BOWED NOT, NOR DID HIM
REVERENCE, THEN WAS HAMAN FULL OF WRATH.   ESTHER 3:5

Esther the Queen - Esther

THEN SAID THE KING UNTO HER, WHAT WILT THOU, QUEEN ESTHER? AND WHAT IS THY REQUEST? IT SHALL BE EVEN GIVEN THEE TO THE HALF OF THE KINGDOM.   ESTHER 5:3

THE STORY OF JOB

AND THE LORD SAID UNTO SATAN, HAST THOU CONSIDERED MY SERVANT JOB, THAT THERE IS NONE LIKE HIM IN THE EARTH, A PERFECT AND AN UPRIGHT MAN, ONE THAT FEARETH GOD . . . ?   JOB 1:8

The Story of Job - Job

AND THE LORD SAID UNTO SATAN, BEHOLD, ALL THAT HE HATH IS IN THY POWER; ONLY UPON HIMSELF PUT NOT FORTH THINE HAND. SO SATAN WENT FORTH FROM THE PRESENCE OF THE LORD.   JOB 1:12

The Story of Job - Job

... WHAT? SHALL WE RECEIVE GOOD AT THE HAND OF GOD, AND SHALL WE NOT RECEIVE EVIL? IN ALL THIS DID NOT JOB SIN WITH HIS LIPS.
JOB 2:10

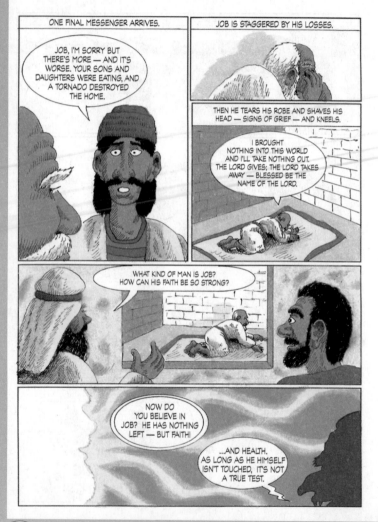

The Story of Job - Job

AND THE LORD TURNED THE CAPTIVITY OF JOB, WHEN HE PRAYED FOR
HIS FRIENDS: ALSO THE LORD GAVE JOB TWICE AS MUCH
AS HE HAD BEFORE.   JOB 42:10

SONGS AND WISDOM

THE LORD IS MY SHEPHERD; I SHALL NOT WANT. HE MAKETH ME TO LIE DOWN IN GREEN PASTURES . . . .   PSALM 23:1-2

ALONG WITH JOB, THE PSALMS, PROVERBS, ECCLESIASTES, AND SONG OF SONGS OFFER WISDOM, MUSIC, AND POETRY FOR GOD'S FAMILY.

PSALMS

THE PSALMS ARE SONGS TO AND ABOUT GOD. DAVID WROTE MANY OF THEM. PSALM 23 TELLS HOW GOD IS LIKE A GOOD SHEPHERD.

THE LORD IS MY SHEPHERD, I SHALL NOT WANT.
HE MAKES ME LIKE DOWN IN GREEN PASTURES,
HE LEADS ME BESIDE THE STILL WATERS,
HE RESTORES MY SOUL...

EVEN THOUGH I WALK THROUGH THE VALLEY
OF THE SHADOW OF DEATH, I WILL FEAR
NO EVIL, FOR YOU ARE WITH ME,
YOUR ROD AND YOUR STAFF, THEY COMFORT ME...

PSALM 1 DESCRIBES THE REWARDS OF OBEYING GOD.

BLESSED IS THE MAN WHO WALKS
NOT IN THE COUNSEL OF THE UNGODLY,
NOR STANDS IN THE WAY OF SINNERS...
BUT HIS DELIGHT IS IN THE LAW
OF THE LORD, AND HE MEDITATES
ON IT DAY AND NIGHT.
AND HE SHALL BE LIKE A TREE
PLANTED BY THE RIVER, THAT
BRINGS FORTH HIS FRUIT IN
HIS SEASON...

MAKE A JOYFUL NOISE UNTO THE LORD, ALL YE LANDS. SERVE THE LORD WITH GLADNESS: COME BEFORE HIS PRESENCE WITH SINGING. PSALM 100:1-2

PSALM 100 CALLS FOR US TO WORSHIP AND PRAISE GOD TOGETHER.

MAKE A JOYFUL NOISE TO THE LORD, ALL THE EARTH. SERVE THE LORD WITH GLADNESS COME BEFORE HIM WITH JOYFUL SONGS, KNOW THAT THE LORD IS GOD. IT'S HE WHO MAKES US, AND NOT WE OURSELVES. WE ARE HIS PEOPLE, THE SHEEP OF HIS PASTURE. ENTER HIS GATES WITH THANKSGIVING AND HIS COURTS WITH PRAISE...

IN PSALM 51, DAVID ASKS GOD TO CLEANSE HIM OF HIS SIN.

...CREATE IN ME A CLEAN HEART, O GOD; RENEW A RIGHT SPIRIT WITHIN ME. CAST ME NOT AWAY FROM YOUR PRESENCE; AND TAKE NOT YOUR HOLY SPIRIT FROM ME.

RESTORE UNTO ME THE JOY OF YOUR SALVATION...

O LORD, OPEN MY LIPS, AND MY MOUTH WILL DECLARE YOUR PRAISE...

PSALM 8 CELEBRATES THE BEAUTY OF GOD'S CREATION.

O LORD, OUR LORD, HOW MAJESTIC IS YOUR NAME IN ALL THE EARTH...

WHEN I CONSIDER THE HEAVENS, THE WORK OF YOUR FINGERS, THE MOON AND THE STARS WHICH YOU SET IN PLACE, WHAT IS MAN, THAT YOU ARE MINDFUL OF HIM?...

O LORD, OUR LORD, HOW EXCELLENT IS YOUR NAME IN ALL THE EARTH!

Songs and Wisdom - Books of Wisdom

TO KNOW WISDOM AND INSTRUCTION; TO PERCEIVE THE WORDS OF
UNDERSTANDING; TO RECEIVE THE INSTRUCTION OF WISDOM, JUSTICE,
AND JUDGMENT, AND EQUITY.   PROVERBS 1:2-3

THE PROVERBS OFFER WISE ADVICE FOR EVERYDAY LIVING. SOLOMON WROTE MANY OF THEM.

THE FEAR OF THE LORD IS THE BEGINNING OF WISDOM. (1:7)

TRUST IN THE LORD WITH ALL YOUR HEART, AND LEAN NOT ON YOUR OWN UNDERSTANDING. IN ALL YOUR WAYS ACKNOWLEDGE HIM, AND HE WILL MAKE STRAIGHT YOUR PATH. (3:5-6)

A GOSSIP BETRAYS A CONFIDENCE, BUT A TRUSTWORTHY MAN KEEPS A SECRET. (11:13)

BLESSED IS HE WHO IS KIND TO THE NEEDY. (14:21)

A GENTLE ANSWER TURNS AWAY WRATH, BUT A HARSH WORD STIRS UP ANGER. (15:1)

A HAPPY HEART MAKES A CHEERFUL FACE. (15:13)

A FRIEND LOVES AT ALL TIMES. (17:17)

LAZINESS BRINGS ON DEEP SLEEP, AND THE SHIFTLESS MAN GOES HUNGRY. (19:15)

TRAIN A CHILD IN THE WAY HE SHOULD GO, AND WHEN HE IS OLDER HE WILL NOT DEPART FROM IT. (22:6)

LET US HEAR THE CONCLUSION OF THE WHOLE MATTER: FEAR GOD, AND
KEEP HIS COMMANDMENTS: FOR THIS IS THE WHOLE DUTY OF MAN.
ECCLESIASTES 12:13

WHY IS LIFE SO OFTEN UNHAPPY? THE WRITER OF
ECCLESIASTES SHOWS THAT OBEYING GOD MAKES LIFE MEANINGFUL.

THERE IS A TIME FOR EVERYTHING, AND A SEASON
UNDER HEAVEN FOR EVERY ACTIVITY.

A TIME TO BE BORN, AND
A TIME TO DIE,
A TIME TO PLANT AND
A TIME TO UPROOT...
A TIME TO WEEP AND
A TIME TO LAUGH...
A TIME TO BE SILENT AND
A TIME TO SPEAK...
A TIME FOR WAR AND
A TIME FOR PEACE...
(FROM CHAPTER 3)

NOW IT HAS ALL BEEN HEARD; HERE IS THE CONCLUSION:
FEAR GOD AND KEEP HIS COMMANDMENTS,
FOR THIS IS THE WHOLE DUTY OF MAN. (12:13)

THE SONG OF SONGS SHOWS THE LOVE BETWEEN HUSBAND
AND WIFE — AND OUR LOVE TO GOD.

LOVE BURNS LIKE
A ROARING FIRE,
LIKE A MIGHTY FLAME.
MANY WATERS
CANNOT QUENCH LOVE;
RIVERS CANNOT WASH
IT AWAY.

IF ONE WERE TO GIVE
ALL THE WEALTH
OF ONE'S HOUSE FOR LOVE,
IT WOULD BE COMPLETELY
SCORNED.

ISAIAH AND JEREMIAH

ALSO I HEARD THE VOICE OF THE LORD, SAYING, WHOM SHALL I SEND,
AND WHO WILL GO FOR US? THEN SAID I, HERE AM I; SEND ME.
ISAIAH 6:8

Isaiah and Jeremiah - Isaiah and Jeremiah

FOR UNTO US A CHILD IS BORN, UNTO US A SON IS GIVEN: AND THE
GOVERNMENT SHALL BE UPON HIS SHOULDER: AND HIS NAME SHALL BE
CALLED WONDERFUL, COUNSELLOR . . . .   ISAIAH 9:6

BEFORE I FORMED THEE IN THE BELLY I KNEW THEE; AND BEFORE THOU CAMEST FORTH OUT OF THE WOMB I SANCTIFIED THEE, AND I ORDAINED THEE A PROPHET UNTO THE NATIONS.   JEREMIAH 1:5

Isaiah and Jeremiah - Isaiah and Jeremiah

THE HEART IS DECEITFUL ABOVE ALL THINGS, AND DESPERATELY WICKED: WHO CAN KNOW IT?   JEREMIAH 17:9

THE STORY OF EZEKIEL

AND I LOOKED, AND, BEHOLD, A WHIRLWIND CAME OUT OF THE NORTH, A
GREAT CLOUD, AND A FIRE INFOLDING ITSELF, AND A BRIGHTNESS
WAS ABOUT IT . . . .   EZEKIEL 1:4

The Story of Ezekiel - Ezekiel

AND WHEN THEY WENT, I HEARD THE NOISE OF THEIR WINGS, LIKE THE NOISE OF GREAT WATERS, AS THE VOICE OF THE ALMIGHTY, THE VOICE OF SPEECH, AS THE NOISE OF AN HOST .... EZEKIEL 1:24

EZEKIEL SEES AN INCREDIBLE VISION.

EACH PART OF THE VISION — THE ANIMALS, THE WHEELS, THE THRONE — HAS A MESSAGE FOR EZEKIEL ABOUT THE POWER AND GLORY OF GOD.

The Story of Ezekiel - Ezekiel

THE HAND OF THE LORD WAS UPON ME, AND CARRIED ME OUT IN THE
SPIRIT OF THE LORD, AND SET ME DOWN IN THE MIDST OF THE VALLEY
WHICH WAS FULL OF BONES.   EZEKIEL 37:1

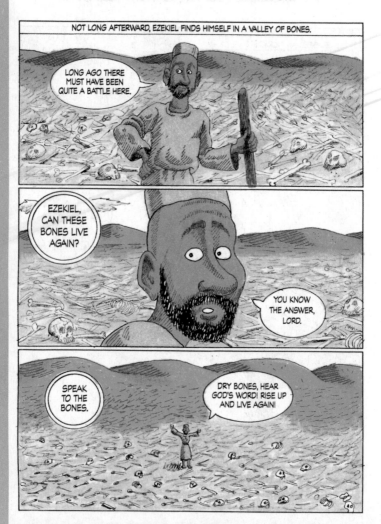

The Story of Ezekiel - Ezekiel

SO I PROPHESIED AS HE COMMANDED ME, AND THE BREATH CAME INTO THEM, AND THEY LIVED, AND STOOD UP UPON THEIR FEET, AN EXCEEDING GREAT ARMY.   EZEKIEL 37:10

The Story of Ezekiel - Ezekiel

THE STORY OF DANIEL

...THESE MEN, O KING, HAVE NOT REGARDED THEE: THEY SERVE NOT THY GODS, NOR WORSHIP THE GOLDEN IMAGE WHICH THOU HAST SET UP.
DANIEL 3:12

DURING THE JEWS' CAPTIVITY IN BABYLON, FAR FROM HOME, DANIEL AND THREE FRIENDS — SHADRACH, MESHACH, AND ABEDNEGO — HOLD IMPORTANT JOBS UNDER THE KING, WHO HOLDS THEM IN RESPECT.

HOW CAN WE BE TRUE TO GOD WHILE SERVING AN UNBELIEVING KING?

JUST HAVE FAITH AND OBEY THE LORD.

KING NEBUCHADNEZZAR ISSUES AN ORDER.

KING NEBUCHADNEZZAR ORDERS EVERYONE TO BOW BEFORE THIS NEW IDOL.

KING, THREE MEN — ALL HEBREWS — REFUSED TO KNEEL!

WHAT'S THIS? I EXPECT MY LEADERS TO OBEY ME! SUMMON THEM!

HE ANSWERED AND SAID, LO, I SEE FOUR MEN LOOSE, WALKING IN THE MIDST OF THE FIRE, AND THEY HAVE NO HURT; AND THE FORM OF THE FOURTH IS LIKE THE SON OF GOD.   DANIEL 3:25

THEN THE KING COMMANDED, AND THEY BROUGHT DANIEL, AND CAST
HIM INTO THE DEN OF LIONS ....   DANIEL 6:16

The Story of Daniel - Daniel

MY GOD HATH SENT HIS ANGEL, AND HATH SHUT THE LIONS' MOUTHS,
THAT THEY HAVE NOT HURT ME: FORASMUCH AS BEFORE HIM INNOCENCY
WAS FOUND IN ME . . . .   DANIEL 6:22

The Story of Daniel - Daniel

THE STORY OF JONAH

ARISE, GO TO NINEVEH, THAT GREAT CITY, AND CRY AGAINST IT; FOR THEIR WICKEDNESS IS COME UP BEFORE ME.   JONAH 1:2

SO THEY TOOK UP JONAH, AND CAST HIM FORTH INTO THE SEA: AND THE
SEA CEASED FROM HER RAGING.   JONAH 1:15

AND [JONAH] SAID, I CRIED BY REASON OF MINE AFFLICTION UNTO THE LORD, AND HE HEARD ME; OUT OF THE BELLY OF HELL CRIED I, AND THOU HEARDEST MY VOICE.   JONAH 2:2

The Story of Jonah - Jonah

BUT LET MAN AND BEAST BE COVERED WITH SACKCLOTH, AND CRY MIGHTILY UNTO GOD: YEA, LET THEM TURN EVERY ONE FROM HIS EVIL WAY, AND FROM THE VIOLENCE THAT IS IN THEIR HANDS.   JONAH 3:8

THE MINOR PROPHETS

ALAS FOR THE DAY! FOR THE DAY OF THE LORD IS AT HAND, AND AS A DESTRUCTION FROM THE ALMIGHTY SHALL IT COME.   JOEL 1:15

TWELVE MEN, INCLUDING JONAH, ARE KNOWN AS MINOR PROPHETS ONLY BECAUSE THE OTHER PROPHETS — ISAIAH, JEREMIAH, EZEKIEL, AND DANIEL — WROTE LONGER BOOKS.

REPENT! TURN BACK TO GOD!

GOD CHOSE THESE MEN TO SPEAK TO JUDAH AND ISRAEL FOR HIM.

HOSEA IS A STORY OF LOVE AND FORGIVENESS. JUST AS THE PROPHET ACCEPTS A WIFE WHO HAS FAILED HIM, SO WILL GOD RESTORE AND FORGIVE ISRAEL.

JOEL WARNS OF THE DAY OF THE LORD, JUDGMENT DAY. BUT HE ALSO PREDICTS A DAY WHEN GOD WILL POUR OUT HIS SPIRIT ON ALL PEOPLE.

THE LORD'S VOICE CRIETH UNTO THE CITY, AND THE MAN OF WISDOM
SHALL SEE THY NAME: HEAR YE THE ROD, AND WHO HATH APPOINTED IT.
MICAH 6:9

AMOS IS A SHEPHERD PREACHING ABOUT JUSTICE. HE WARNS THAT GOD CARES
HOW WE TREAT THE POOR.

PREPARE TO MEET OUR GOD!

OBADIAH HAS A WARNING FOR EDOM. THAT NEIGHBOR REFUSED TO HELP THE JEWS
WHEN JERUSALEM WAS BEING DESTROYED. SO GOD WILL BRING JUDGMENT.

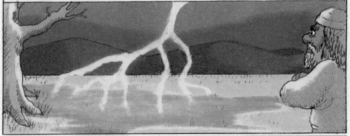

MICAH SPEAKS FOR THE POOR, LIKE AMOS. HE PREACHES AGAINST THEIR MISTREATMENT.
BUT HE ALSO PREDICTS THAT A WONDERFUL CHILD WILL BE BORN IN BETHLEHEM.

THEREFORE THE LAW IS SLACKED, AND JUDGMENT DOTH NEVER GO
FORTH: FOR THE WICKED DOTH COMPASS ABOUT THE RIGHTEOUS;
THEREFORE WRONG JUDGMENT PROCEEDETH.   HABAKKUK 1:4

NAHUM FOLLOWS IN JONAH'S STEPS,
PREACHING IN NINEVEH 150 YEARS LATER.

THEY HAVE ANGERED GOD AGAIN, AND THIS TIME
IT MEANS THEIR DESTRUCTION AT THE
HANDS OF BABYLON.

HABAKKUK ASKS GOD WHY EVIL PEOPLE
GO UNPUNISHED. GOD ANSWERS THAT HE
WILL INDEED PUNISH THE WICKED.

"THE LORD IS IN HIS HOLY TEMPLE. LET ALL
THE EARTH KEEP SILENT BEFORE HIM."

ZEPHANIAH IS A COUSIN OF KING JOSIAH, WHO BRINGS REVIVAL TO JUDAH. THIS
PROPHET HELPS SPREAD THE WORD TO RETURN TO GOD.

REMEMBER YE THE LAW OF MOSES MY SERVANT, WHICH I COMMANDED
UNTO HIM IN HOREB FOR ALL ISRAEL, WITH THE STATUTES
AND JUDGMENTS.   MALACHI 4:4

HAGGAI HAS A PRACTICAL MESSAGE: BUILD THE TEMPLE! AFTER THE RETURN FROM
BABYLON, THIS PROPHET ENCOURAGES THE PEOPLE TO RESTORE THE HOUSE OF GOD.

ZECHARIAH, LIKE HIS FRIEND HAGGAI, PREACHES ABOUT THE TEMPLE — AND OF THE
DAY WHEN THE MESSIAH WILL ENTER JERUSALEM RIDING A YOUNG DONKEY.

MALACHI CLOSES THE OLD TESTAMENT. TO THOSE WHOSE FAITH HAS DIED, MALACHI
SAYS, "GIVE GOD YOUR BEST!"

BUT THE PEOPLE ARE
FURTHER FROM GOD
THAN EVER BEFORE—AND
FOR 400 YEARS HE
WILL BE SILENT.

The Minor Prophets - The Minor Prophets

THE BIRTH OF JESUS

AND MARY SAID, MY SOUL DOTH MAGNIFY THE LORD, AND MY SPIRIT HATH REJOICED IN GOD MY SAVIOUR.   LUKE 1:46-47

AND JOSEPH ALSO WENT UP FROM GALILEE, OUT OF THE CITY OF
NAZARETH, INTO JUDAEA, UNTO THE CITY OF DAVID,
WHICH IS CALLED BETHLEHEM.   LUKE 2:4

AND SHE BROUGHT FORTH HER FIRSTBORN SON, AND WRAPPED HIM IN SWADDLING CLOTHES, AND LAID HIM IN A MANGER; BECAUSE THERE WAS NO ROOM FOR THEM IN THE INN.   LUKE 2:7

AND SUDDENLY THERE WAS WITH THE ANGEL A MULTITUDE OF THE
HEAVENLY HOST PRAISING GOD, AND SAYING, GLORY TO GOD IN THE
HIGHEST, AND ON EARTH PEACE, GOOD WILL TOWARD MEN.
LUKE 2:13-14

LET'S GO SEE THIS AMAZING CHILD!
BETHLEHEM IS JUST AHEAD.

THE TOWN IS QUIET, BUT THEY SEE THE
LIGHT FROM A STABLE.

THERE THEY FIND MARY, JOSEPH, AND A BEAUTIFUL CHILD.

LATER THE
SHEPHERDS
PRAISE GOD AS
THEY TELL
EVERYONE WHAT
THEY HAVE SEEN.

The Birth of Jesus - Luke 1 and 2

THE CHILDHOOD OF JESUS

. . . WHERE IS HE THAT IS BORN KING OF THE JEWS? FOR WE HAVE SEEN HIS STAR IN THE EAST, AND ARE COME TO WORSHIP HIM.

MATTHEW 2:2

THE NIGHT OF JESUS' BIRTH, IN AN EASTERN LAND...

WE'VE STUDIED THE STARS FOR YEARS, AND WE'VE NEVER SEEN ONE LIKE THIS!

IT IS A SIGN THE KING OF THE JEWS HAS COME.

SO THEY TRAVEL TO JERUSALEM.

I, HEROD, AM THE KING...BUT THE CHILD IS TO BE BORN IN BETHLEHEM.

THEN TO BETHLEHEM WE GO.

IF YOU FIND HIM, COME TELL ME...SO I MAY COME WORSHIP HIM, TOO!

The Childhood of Jesus - Matthew 2 and Luke 2

AND WHEN THEY WERE COME INTO THE HOUSE, THEY SAW THE YOUNG
CHILD WITH MARY HIS MOTHER, AND FELL DOWN, AND WORSHIPPED
HIM: . . .THEY PRESENTED UNTO HIM GIFTS; GOLD, AND FRANKINCENSE,
AND MYRRH.   MATTHEW 2:11

NOW HIS PARENTS WENT TO JERUSALEM EVERY YEAR AT THE FEAST OF THE PASSOVER. AND WHEN HE WAS TWELVE YEARS OLD, THEY WENT UP TO JERUSALEM AFTER THE CUSTOM OF THE FEAST.   LUKE 2:41-42

The Childhood of Jesus - Matthew 2 and Luke 2

AND HE SAID UNTO THEM, HOW IS IT THAT YE SOUGHT ME? WIST YE NOT THAT I MUST BE ABOUT MY FATHER'S BUSINESS?   LUKE 2:49

The Childhood of Jesus - Matthew 2 and Luke 2

THE BAPTISM OF JESUS

AND HE CAME INTO ALL THE COUNTRY ABOUT JORDAN, PREACHING THE BAPTISM OF REPENTANCE FOR THE REMISSION OF SINS.   LUKE 3:3

... I INDEED BAPTIZE YOU WITH WATER; BUT ONE MIGHTIER THAN I COMETH, THE LATCHET OF WHOSE SHOES I AM NOT WORTHY TO UNLOOSE .... LUKE 3:16

NO PROPHET IS WELCOME IN HIS HOMETOWN. REMEMBER HOW ELIJAH WAS TREATED?

HE'S COMPARING US TO THOSE WHO ABUSED THE PROPHETS? DRIVE HIM OUT!

FURIOUS ABOUT THE VERY WORDS THEY ARE PROVING TRUE, THE MEN CHASE JESUS TO THE TOP OF A HILL.

BUT HE CALMLY PASSES THROUGH THE CROWD AND WALKS AWAY.

JESUS LEAVES HIS HOMETOWN.

The Baptism of Jesus - Luke 3

AND THE HOLY GHOST DESCENDED IN A BODILY SHAPE LIKE A DOVE UPON HIM, AND A VOICE CAME FROM HEAVEN, WHICH SAID, THOU ART MY BELOVED SON; IN THEE I AM WELL PLEASED.   LUKE 3:22

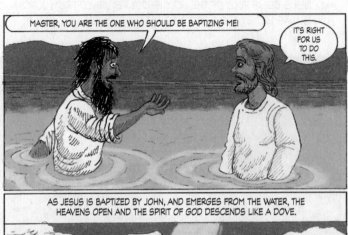

The Baptism of Jesus - Luke 3

JESUS IS TEMPTED

AND JESUS BEING FULL OF THE HOLY GHOST RETURNED FROM JORDAN,
AND WAS LED BY THE SPIRIT INTO THE WILDERNESS.   LUKE 4:1

JESUS, FILLED WITH THE SPIRIT OF GOD, RETURNS FROM JORDAN.

THE SAME SPIRIT IMMEDIATELY LEADS JESUS DEEP INTO THE DESERT.

FOR 40 DAYS, HE IS ALONE IN THE DESERT. HAVING EATEN NOTHING, HE GROWS HUNGRY.

AND JESUS ANSWERED AND SAID UNTO HIM, GET THEE BEHIND ME, SATAN: FOR IT IS WRITTEN, THOU SHALT WORSHIP THE LORD THY GOD, AND HIM ONLY SHALT THOU SERVE.   LUKE 4:8

AND JESUS ANSWERING SAID UNTO HIM, IT IS SAID, THOU SHALT NOT TEMPT THE LORD THY GOD. AND WHEN THE DEVIL HAD ENDED ALL THE TEMPTATION, HE DEPARTED FROM HIM FOR A SEASON.   LUKE 4:12-13

Jesus Is Tempted - Luke 4

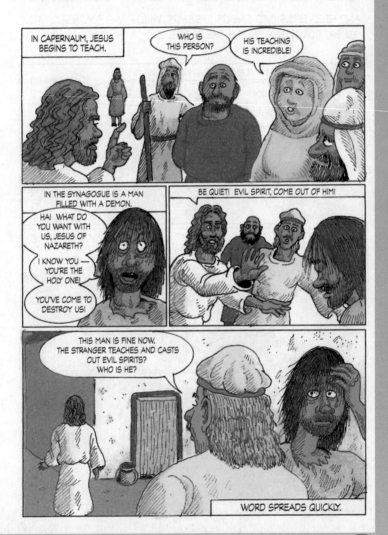

Jesus Is Tempted - Luke 4

JESUS FINDS DISCIPLES

AND HE ENTERED INTO ONE OF THE SHIPS, WHICH WAS SIMON'S, . . . AND HE SAT DOWN, AND TAUGHT THE PEOPLE OUT OF THE SHIP.   LUKE 5:3

Jesus Finds Disciples - Luke 5 and John 3

NOW WHEN HE HAD LEFT SPEAKING, HE SAID UNTO SIMON, LAUNCH OUT
INTO THE DEEP, AND LET DOWN YOUR NETS FOR A DRAUGHT.
LUKE 5:4

AND WHEN IT WAS DAY, HE CALLED UNTO HIM HIS DISCIPLES: AND OF
THEM HE CHOSE TWELVE, WHOM ALSO HE NAMED APOSTLES.
LUKE 6:13

Jesus Finds Disciples - Luke 5 and John 3

FOR GOD SO LOVED THE WORLD, THAT HE GAVE HIS ONLY BEGOTTEN SON, THAT WHOSOEVER BELIEVETH IN HIM SHOULD NOT PERISH, BUT HAVE EVERLASTING LIFE.   JOHN 3:16

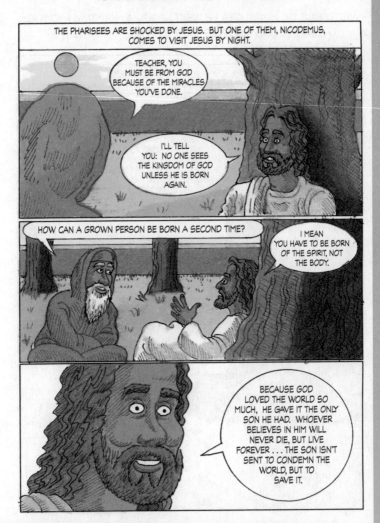

JESUS TEACHES PEOPLE

AND SEEING THE MULTITUDES, HE WENT UP INTO A MOUNTAIN: AND WHEN HE WAS SET, HIS DISCIPLES CAME UNTO HIM.   MATTHEW 5:1

CROWDS BEGIN TO FOLLOW JESUS WHEREVER HE GOES. SO, AT THE MOUNTAINSIDE, HE SITS AND BEGINS TO TEACH HIS DISCIPLES.

BLESSED ARE THE POOR IN SPIRIT, FOR THEIRS IS THE KINGDOM OF HEAVEN. BLESSED ARE THOSE WHO MOURN, FOR THEY WILL BE COMFORTED.

THESE TEACHINGS ARE KNOWN AS THE SERMON ON THE MOUNT OR THE BEATITUDES.

LET YOUR LIGHT SO SHINE BEFORE MEN, THAT THEY MAY SEE YOUR
GOOD WORKS, AND GLORIFY YOUR FATHER WHICH IS IN HEAVEN.
MATTHEW 5:16

"YOU ARE THE SALT OF THE EARTH,"
HE CONTINUES.

SALT MAKES PEOPLE THIRSTY — AND
JESUS BRINGS LIVING WATER.

"YOU ARE THE LIGHT OF THE WORLD.
A CITY ON A HILL IS EASY TO SEE —
SO LET YOUR LIGHT SHINE BEFORE MEN."

"YOU'VE HEARD IT IS WRONG TO KILL
PEOPLE. BUT I SAY WHEN YOU BURN
WITH ANGER, IT IS LIKE MURDER."

"YOU'VE HEARD 'AN EYE FOR AN EYE.' BUT
I TELL YOU NOT TO FIGHT EVIL WITH
EVIL. IF SOMEONE STRIKES YOU ON
THE CHEEK, OFFER THE OTHER ONE."

BUT WHEN YE PRAY, USE NOT VAIN REPETITIONS, AS THE HEATHEN DO:
FOR THEY THINK THAT THEY SHALL BE HEARD FOR THEIR
MUCH SPEAKING.   MATTHEW 6:7

THEN JESUS TEACHES THEM TO PRAY.

OUR FATHER,
WHO ART IN HEAVEN,
HALLOWED BE THY NAME.
THY KINGDOM COME,
THY WILL BE DONE,
ON EARTH AS IT IS
IN HEAVEN.
GIVE US THIS DAY
OUR DAILY BREAD,
AND FORGIVE US OUR
DEBTS, AS WE WOULD
FORGIVE OUR DEBTORS.
LEAD US NOT INTO
TEMPTATION,
BUT DELIVER US FROM EVIL.
FOR THINE IS THE
KINGDOM,
AND THE POWER,
AND THE GLORY

FOREVER.

AMEN.

THEREFORE WHOSOEVER HEARETH THESE SAYINGS OF MINE, AND DOETH THEM, I WILL LIKEN HIM UNTO A WISE MAN, WHICH BUILT HIS HOUSE UPON A ROCK.   MATTHEW 7:24

JESUS TEACHES ABOUT WORRYING.

"DON'T WORRY ABOUT WHAT YOU'LL EAT OR WEAR. LIFE IS MORE IMPORTANT THAN FOOD OR CLOTHING. LOOK AT THE BIRDS: THEY DON'T WORRY, YET SOLOMON IN ALL HIS GLORY WASN'T DRESSED AS BEAUTIFULLY."

"AND DO NOT JUDGE OTHERS. GOD WILL JUDGE YOU JUST THE WAY YOU JUDGE OTHERS."

"IF YOU LISTEN TO THESE WORDS AND FOLLOW THEM, YOU'RE LIKE A MAN WHO BUILDS HIS HOUSE ON THE ROCK — IT WILL STAND AGAINST WIND AND STORMS. BUT IF YOU IGNORE MY WORDS, YOU'RE LIKE THE MAN WHO BUILT HIS HOUSE ON THE SAND. WHEN THE WIND AND STORMS CAME, HIS HOUSE FELL WITH A CRASH."

JESUS HEALS PEOPLE

. . . DAUGHTER, BE OF GOOD COMFORT; THY FAITH HATH MADE THEE WHOLE. AND THE WOMAN WAS MADE WHOLE FROM THAT HOUR.
MATTHEW 9:22

AND WHEN HE SAW THEM, HE SAID UNTO THEM, GO SHEW YOURSELVES UNTO THE PRIESTS. AND IT CAME TO PASS, THAT, AS THEY WENT, THEY WERE CLEANSED. LUKE 17:14

... THEY UNCOVERED THE ROOF WHERE HE WAS: AND WHEN THEY HAD BROKEN IT UP, THEY LET DOWN THE BED WHEREIN THE SICK OF THE PALSY LAY.   MARK 2:4

BUT THE MEN ARE DETERMINED, SO THEY CLIMB TO THE ROOF AND LOWER THE SICK MAN THROUGH AN OPENING.

Jesus Heals People - Luke 5

I SAY UNTO THEE, ARISE, AND TAKE UP THY BED, AND GO THY WAY INTO THINE HOUSE. AND IMMEDIATELY HE AROSE, TOOK UP THE BED, AND WENT FORTH BEFORE THEM ALL . . . .   MARK 2:11-12

JESUS AND THE CHILDREN

THEN WERE THERE BROUGHT UNTO HIM LITTLE CHILDREN, THAT HE
SHOULD PUT HIS HANDS ON THEM, AND PRAY: AND THE DISCIPLES
REBUKED THEM.   MATTHEW 19:13

AS THE WORD SPREADS OF JESUS' HEALING POWER, THE CROWDS GROW. IT SEEMS
THAT EVERYONE WANTS TO BE WITH JESUS.

JESUS! CAN YOU BLESS MY CHILDREN?

PLEASE, PEOPLE, LET JESUS PASS! HE IS TOO BUSY FOR CHILDREN!

BUT JESUS SAID, SUFFER LITTLE CHILDREN, AND FORBID THEM NOT, TO COME UNTO ME: FOR OF SUCH IS THE KINGDOM OF HEAVEN.
MATTHEW 19:14

LET THE LITTLE CHILDREN COME TO ME. DON'T BLOCK THEM — THE KINGDOM OF GOD BELONGS TO THEIR TYPE.

HERE'S THE TRUTH: ANYONE WHO DOESN'T RECEIVE GOD'S KINGDOM LIKE ONE OF THESE CHILDREN WILL NEVER ENTER IT.

FROM A MOUNTAINSIDE JESUS SEES A CROWD OF 5,000 PEOPLE GATHERING.

PHILIP, WHERE CAN WE BUY BREAD FOR A CROWD LIKE THIS?

YOU COULD WORK 8 MONTHS AND NOT EARN ENOUGH TO FEED THEM!

Jesus and the Children - Mark 10 and John 6

THERE IS A LAD HERE, WHICH HATH FIVE BARLEY LOAVES, AND TWO SMALL FISHES: BUT WHAT ARE THEY AMONG SO MANY?   JOHN 6:9

Jesus and the Children - Mark 10 and John 6

THEN THOSE MEN, WHEN THEY HAD SEEN THE MIRACLE THAT JESUS DID, SAID, THIS IS OF A TRUTH THAT PROPHET THAT SHOULD COME INTO THE WORLD.   JOHN 6:14

MIRACULOUSLY, 5,000 PEOPLE EAT THEIR FULL!

LET'S NOT WASTE. GATHER WHAT IS LEFT.

THE DISCIPLES GATHER 12 BASKETS OF LEFTOVER FOOD.

CAN YOU BELIEVE WHAT HAPPENED?

THIS IS THE KING FROM THE OLD PROPHECIES! WE'LL RAISE AN ARMY AND OVERPOWER THE ROMANS!

BUT JESUS IS NOT INTERESTED IN KINGS AND ARMIES, AND HE GOES TO THE MOUNTAIN ALONE.

JESUS WALKS ON WATER

AND WHEN HE HAD SENT THE MULTITUDES AWAY, HE WENT UP INTO A
MOUNTAIN APART TO PRAY: AND WHEN THE EVENING WAS COME,
HE WAS THERE ALONE.   MATTHEW 14:23

JESUS HAS FED 5,000, AND NOW HE INSTRUCTS HIS DISCIPLES.

TAKE THE BOAT AND GO TO THE OTHER SHORE WHILE I DISMISS THESE PEOPLE.

WHEN EVERYONE IS GONE, JESUS GOES TO THE MOUNTAINSIDE TO SPEND TIME ALONE
WITH GOD.

BUT THE SHIP WAS NOW IN THE MIDST OF THE SEA, TOSSED WITH WAVES: FOR THE WIND WAS CONTRARY.   MATTHEW 14:24

Jesus Walks on Water - Matthew 14

AND WHEN THE DISCIPLES SAW HIM WALKING ON THE SEA, THEY WERE
TROUBLED, SAYING, IT IS A SPIRIT; AND THEY CRIED OUT FOR FEAR.
MATTHEW 14:26

Jesus Walks on Water - Matthew 14

AND IMMEDIATELY JESUS STRETCHED FORTH HIS HAND, AND CAUGHT HIM, AND SAID UNTO HIM, O THOU OF LITTLE FAITH, WHEREFORE DIDST THOU DOUBT?   MATTHEW 14:31

Jesus Walks on Water - Matthew 14

JESUS TELLS PARABLES

...A CERTAIN MAN WENT DOWN FROM JERUSALEM TO JERICHO, AND FELL AMONG THIEVES, WHICH STRIPPED HIM OF HIS RAIMENT, AND WOUNDED HIM, AND DEPARTED.   LUKE 10:30

JESUS TEACHES ABOUT GOD BY TELLING STORIES CALLED PARABLES.

A MAN WAS TRAVELING FROM JERUSALEM DOWN TO JERICHO. THIEVES CAUGHT UP WITH HIM. THEY BEAT HIM, ROBBED HIM, AND LEFT HIM FOR DEAD.

"THE GOOD SAMARITAN"

"A PRIEST HAPPENED TO PASS BY, SAW THE WOUNDED FELLOW, AND WALKED ON BY."

BUT A CERTAIN SAMARITAN, AS HE JOURNEYED, CAME WHERE HE WAS: AND WHEN HE SAW HIM, HE HAD COMPASSION ON HIM.   LUKE 10:33

AND NOT MANY DAYS AFTER THE YOUNGER SON GATHERED ALL TOGETHER, AND TOOK HIS JOURNEY INTO A FAR COUNTRY, AND THERE WASTED HIS SUBSTANCE WITH RIOTOUS LIVING.   LUKE 15:13

Jesus Tells Parables - Luke 10 and 15

FOR THIS MY SON WAS DEAD, AND IS ALIVE AGAIN; HE WAS LOST, AND IS FOUND. AND THEY BEGAN TO BE MERRY.   LUKE 15:24

JESUS AND ZACCHAEUS

AND A CERTAIN RULER ASKED HIM, SAYING, GOOD MASTER, WHAT SHALL I DO TO INHERIT ETERNAL LIFE?   LUKE 18:18

Jesus and Zacchaeus - Luke 19

AND, BEHOLD, THERE WAS A MAN NAMED ZACCHAEUS, WHICH WAS THE CHIEF AMONG THE PUBLICANS, AND HE WAS RICH. AND HE SOUGHT TO SEE JESUS WHO HE WAS .... LUKE 19:2-3

AND WHEN JESUS CAME TO THE PLACE, HE LOOKED UP, AND SAW HIM, AND SAID UNTO HIM, ZACCHAEUS, MAKE HASTE, AND COME DOWN; FOR TO DAY I MUST ABIDE AT THY HOUSE.   LUKE 19:5

AND ZACCHAEUS STOOD, AND SAID UNTO THE LORD; BEHOLD, LORD, THE
HALF OF MY GOODS I GIVE TO THE POOR . . . .   LUKE 19:8

JESUS RAISES LAZARUS

THEREFORE HIS SISTERS SENT UNTO HIM, SAYING, LORD, BEHOLD, HE WHOM THOU LOVEST IS SICK.   JOHN 11:3

... HE SAITH UNTO THEM, OUR FRIEND LAZARUS SLEEPETH; BUT I GO, THAT I MAY AWAKE HIM OUT OF SLEEP.   JOHN 11:11

Jesus Raises Lazarus - John 11

JESUS SAID UNTO HER, I AM THE RESURRECTION, AND THE LIFE: HE THAT BELIEVETH IN ME, THOUGH HE WERE DEAD, YET SHALL HE LIVE.
JOHN 11:25

Jesus Raises Lazarus - John 11

AND WHEN HE THUS HAD SPOKEN, HE CRIED WITH A LOUD VOICE, LAZARUS, COME FORTH. AND HE THAT WAS DEAD CAME FORTH, BOUND HAND AND FOOT WITH GRAVECLOTHES .... JOHN 11:43-44

Jesus Raises Lazarus - John 11

JESUS IN JERUSALEM

...GO YOUR WAY INTO THE VILLAGE OVER AGAINST YOU: AND AS SOON AS YE BE ENTERED INTO IT, YE SHALL FIND A COLT TIED, WHEREON NEVER MAN SAT; LOOSE HIM, AND BRING HIM.   MARK 11:2

AND MANY SPREAD THEIR GARMENTS IN THE WAY: AND OTHERS CUT
DOWN BRANCHES OFF THE TREES, AND STRAWED THEM IN THE WAY.
MARK 11:8

THEY BRING THE DONKEY, AND JESUS ENTERS
JERUSALEM AS CROWDS CHEER FOR HIM.

THEY PUT COATS AND BRANCHES IN THE ROAD TO WELCOME A KING.

Jesus in Jerusalem - Mark 11

AND HE TAUGHT, SAYING UNTO THEM, IS IT NOT WRITTEN, MY HOUSE SHALL BE CALLED OF ALL NATIONS THE HOUSE OF PRAYER? BUT YE HAVE MADE IT A DEN OF THIEVES.   MARK 11:17

... AND JESUS WENT INTO THE TEMPLE, AND BEGAN TO CAST OUT THEM THAT SOLD AND BOUGHT IN THE TEMPLE, AND OVERTHREW THE TABLES OF THE MONEYCHANGERS .... MARK 11:15

JESUS DRIVES OUT THE MONEY-MAKERS, TOPPLING THEIR TABLES.

DID YOU SEE THE WAY THE PEOPLE LISTEN TO HIM?

WE MUST FIND A WAY TO GET RID OF HIM.

Jesus in Jerusalem - Mark 11

JESUS' LAST SUPPER

NOW THE FIRST DAY OF THE FEAST OF UNLEAVENED BREAD THE DISCIPLES CAME TO JESUS, SAYING UNTO HIM, WHERE WILT THOU THAT WE PREPARE FOR THEE TO EAT THE PASSOVER?   MATTHEW 26:17

NOW WHEN THE EVEN WAS COME, HE SAT DOWN WITH THE TWELVE. AND AS THEY DID EAT, HE SAID, VERILY I SAY UNTO YOU, THAT ONE OF YOU SHALL BETRAY ME.   MATTHEW 26:20-21

JESUS SAID UNTO HIM, VERILY I SAY UNTO THEE, THAT THIS NIGHT, BEFORE THE COCK CROW, THOU SHALT DENY ME THRICE.   MATTHEW 26:34

AND JESUS SAID UNTO HIM, FRIEND, WHEREFORE ART THOU COME? THEN CAME THEY, AND LAID HANDS ON JESUS, AND TOOK HIM.
MATTHEW 26:50

JESUS IS CRUCIFIED

AND JESUS STOOD BEFORE THE GOVERNOR: AND THE GOVERNOR ASKED HIM, SAYING, ART THOU THE KING OF THE JEWS? AND JESUS SAID UNTO HIM, THOU SAYEST.   MATTHEW 27:11

JESUS APPEARS BEFORE THE ELDERS AND HIGH PRIEST.

I COMMAND YOU UNDER OATH TO TELL US: ARE YOU THE SON OF GOD?

IT IS AS YOU SAY. AND IN THE FUTURE YOU WILL SEE THE SON OF MAN COMING ON THE CLOUDS, AND SITTING AT GOD'S RIGHT HAND.

BLASPHEMY!

HE DESERVES DEATH!

HAND HIM OVER TO THE ROMANS!

OUT IN THE COURTYARD, PETER IS NOTICED.

YOU'RE ONE OF JESUS' MEN.

I DON'T KNOW WHAT YOU'RE TALKING ABOUT.

IN FEAR, PETER DENIES HE KNOWS JESUS — JUST AS JESUS PREDICTED.

THEN SAID PILATE UNTO HIM, HEAREST THOU NOT HOW MANY THINGS THEY WITNESS AGAINST THEE? AND HE ANSWERED HIM TO NEVER A WORD; INSOMUCH THAT THE GOVERNOR MARVELLED GREATLY.
MATTHEW 27:13-14

JUDAS SEES HOW JESUS IS TREATED AND IS FILLED WITH HORROR.

HE THROWS THE MONEY DOWN, AND TAKES HIS OWN LIFE.

JESUS THEN APPEARS BEFORE PILATE, THE ROMAN GOVERNOR.

ARE YOU THE KING OF THE JEWS?

YES, IT IS AS YOU SAY.

THE CHIEF PRIESTS AND ELDERS YELL INSULTS, BUT JESUS STANDS SILENTLY.

THERE IS AN OLD TRADITION THAT THE GOVERNOR MAY RELEASE ONE PRISONER ON THE PASSOVER FEAST. PILATE WANTS TO AVOID EXECUTING JESUS, SO HE ASKS THE CROWD IF JESUS MIGHT BE RELEASED.

NO! FREE THE OTHER ONE!

BARABBAS!

GIVE US BARABBAS!

DEATH TO JESUS!

BARABBAS, A MURDERER, IS SET FREE INSTEAD.

AND AFTER THAT THEY HAD MOCKED HIM, THEY TOOK THE ROBE OFF FROM HIM, AND PUT HIS OWN RAIMENT ON HIM, AND LED HIM AWAY TO CRUCIFY HIM.   MATTHEW 27:31

THE SOLDIERS MOCK JESUS, PUTTING A RED ROBE AND A PAINFUL CROWN OF THORNS ON HIM. THEY SPIT ON HIM AND BEAT HIM.

HAIL, KING OF THE JEWS!

JESUS IS SENTENCED TO DEATH. HE IS FALSELY ACCUSED OF BEING A TROUBLEMAKER, AND OF SPEAKING BLASPHEMY AGAINST GOD. THE ROMANS EXECUTE CRIMINALS BY NAILING THEM TO WOODEN CROSSES.

THEY FORCE JESUS TO CARRY HIS OWN CROSSBAR.

NOW WHEN THE CENTURION, AND THEY THAT WERE WITH HIM, WATCHING JESUS, SAW THE EARTHQUAKE, AND THOSE THINGS THAT WERE DONE, THEY FEARED GREATLY, SAYING, TRULY THIS WAS THE SON OF GOD. MATTHEW 27:54

JESUS IS RISEN!

THE FIRST DAY OF THE WEEK COMETH MARY MAGDALENE EARLY, WHEN IT WAS YET DARK, UNTO THE SEPULCHRE, AND SEETH THE STONE TAKEN AWAY FROM THE SEPULCHRE.   JOHN 20:1

NICODEMUS, A PHARISEE WHO HAD VISITED JESUS, AND JOSEPH OF ARIMATHEA ASK FOR JESUS' BODY. THEY WRAP IT BY JEWISH CUSTOM AND BURY HIM.

ON SUNDAY MORNING, MARY MAGDALENE VISITS THE TOMB WHILE IT IS STILL DARK.

BUT... THE STONE IS ROLLED AWAY!

THEN SHE RUNNETH, AND COMETH TO SIMON PETER ... THEY HAVE TAKEN AWAY THE LORD OUT OF THE SEPULCHRE, AND WE KNOW NOT WHERE THEY HAVE LAID HIM.   JOHN 20:2

AND THEY SAY UNTO HER, WOMAN, WHY WEEPEST THOU? SHE SAITH UNTO THEM, BECAUSE THEY HAVE TAKEN AWAY MY LORD, AND I KNOW NOT WHERE THEY HAVE LAID HIM.   JOHN 20:13

AFTER PETER AND JOHN LEAVE, MARY REMAINS BY THE TOMB, CRYING. FINALLY SHE LOOKS INSIDE. TWO ANGELS ARE SITTING WHERE JESUS WAS.

WOMAN, WHY ARE YOU CRYING?

BECAUSE THEY HAVE TAKEN MY LORD AWAY.

SHE TURNS AND SEES JESUS — BUT SHE DOES NOT RECOGNIZE HIM.

PLEASE, SIR... IF YOU'VE CARRIED THE BODY AWAY, TELL ME WHERE IT IS.

MARY.

SUDDENLY MARY KNOWS IT IS JESUS. HE SENDS HER TO TELL THE DISCIPLES.

JESUS SAITH UNTO HIM, THOMAS, BECAUSE THOU HAST SEEN ME, THOU HAST BELIEVED: BLESSED ARE THEY THAT HAVE NOT SEEN, AND YET HAVE BELIEVED.   JOHN 20:29

PETER IS FORGIVEN

PETER THEN DENIED AGAIN: AND IMMEDIATELY THE COCK CREW.
JOHN 18:27

PETER IS FILLED WITH MEMORIES OF JESUS.

PETER REMEMBERS STEPPING OUT OF THE BOAT AND — JUST FOR A MOMENT — WALKING WITH JESUS.

WHO DO YOU SAY THAT I AM?

YOU ARE THE CHRIST — SON OF THE LIVING GOD!

THE OTHERS MAY FALL AWAY, BUT NEVER ME, LORD!

I'M NOT A FRIEND OF JESUS! YOU'VE MISTAKEN ME FOR SOMEONE ELSE!

... CAST THE NET ON THE RIGHT SIDE OF THE SHIP, AND YE SHALL FIND. THEY CAST THEREFORE, AND NOW THEY WERE NOT ABLE TO DRAW IT FOR THE MULTITUDE OF FISHES.   JOHN 21:6

. . . NOW WHEN SIMON PETER HEARD THAT IT WAS THE LORD, HE GIRT HIS FISHER'S COAT UNTO HIM, (FOR HE WAS NAKED,) AND DID CAST HIMSELF INTO THE SEA.   JOHN 21:7

JOHN IS THE FIRST TO RECOGNIZE THE STRANGER.

IT IS THE LORD!

PETER LEAPS FROM THE BOAT AND SWIMS TO SHORE.

BRING SOME OF YOUR FISH AND WE'LL FIX BREAKFAST.

... JESUS SAITH TO SIMON PETER, SIMON, SON OF JONAS, LOVEST THOU ME MORE THAN THESE? HE SAITH UNTO HIM, YEA, LORD; THOU KNOWEST THAT I LOVE THEE .... JOHN 21:15

JESUS SENDS THE SPIRIT

AND THAT REPENTANCE AND REMISSION OF SINS SHOULD BE PREACHED
IN HIS NAME AMONG ALL NATIONS, BEGINNING AT JERUSALEM.
LUKE 24:47

. . . HE LIFTED UP HIS HANDS, AND BLESSED THEM. AND IT CAME TO PASS, WHILE HE BLESSED THEM, HE WAS PARTED FROM THEM, AND CARRIED UP INTO HEAVEN.   LUKE 24:50-51

AND SUDDENLY THERE CAME A SOUND FROM HEAVEN AS OF A RUSHING MIGHTY WIND, AND IT FILLED ALL THE HOUSE WHERE THEY WERE SITTING. ACTS 2:2

LATER, THE DISCIPLES MEET IN A ROOM TO CHOOSE A REPLACEMENT FOR JUDAS.

WELCOME, MATTHIAS — YOU ARE ONE OF THE TWELVE!

ON THE HEBREW DAY OF PENTECOST, JESUS' WORDS COME TRUE. A RUSHING WIND IS HEARD, AND TONGUES OF FIRE COME TO REST ON EACH DISCIPLE.

THE HOLY SPIRIT HAS ARRIVED! THE DISCIPLES BEGIN TO SPEAK IN THE LANGUAGES OF OTHER LANDS.

... REPENT, AND BE BAPTIZED EVERY ONE OF YOU IN THE NAME OF JESUS CHRIST FOR THE REMISSION OF SINS, AND YE SHALL RECEIVE THE GIFT OF THE HOLY GHOST.   ACTS 2:38

THE FIRST CHRISTIANS

AND STEPHEN, FULL OF FAITH AND POWER, DID GREAT WONDERS AND MIRACLES AMONG THE PEOPLE.   ACTS 6:8

The First Christians - Acts 6 through 8

AND THEY STIRRED UP THE PEOPLE, AND THE ELDERS, AND THE SCRIBES, AND CAME UPON HIM, AND CAUGHT HIM, AND BROUGHT HIM TO THE COUNCIL.   ACTS 6:12

AND HE KNEELED DOWN, AND CRIED WITH A LOUD VOICE, LORD, LAY NOT THIS SIN TO THEIR CHARGE. AND WHEN HE HAD SAID THIS, HE FELL ASLEEP.   ACTS 7:60

The First Christians - Acts 6 through 8

AS FOR SAUL, HE MADE HAVOCK OF THE CHURCH, ENTERING INTO EVERY
HOUSE, AND HALING MEN AND WOMEN COMMITTED THEM TO PRISON.
ACTS 8:3

PAUL MEETS CHRIST

AND SAUL, YET BREATHING OUT THREATENINGS AND SLAUGHTER
AGAINST THE DISCIPLES OF THE LORD, WENT UNTO THE HIGH PRIEST, AND
DESIRED OF HIM LETTERS TO DAMASCUS TO THE SYNAGOGUES . . . .
ACTS 9:1-2

...AND SUDDENLY THERE SHINED ROUND ABOUT HIM A LIGHT FROM HEAVEN: AND HE FELL TO THE EARTH, AND HEARD A VOICE SAYING UNTO HIM, SAUL, SAUL, WHY PERSECUTEST THOU ME?   ACTS 9:3-4

AND SAUL AROSE FROM THE EARTH; AND WHEN HIS EYES WERE OPENED, HE SAW NO MAN: BUT THEY LED HIM BY THE HAND, AND BROUGHT HIM INTO DAMASCUS.   ACTS 9:8

AND IMMEDIATELY THERE FELL FROM HIS EYES AS IT HAD BEEN SCALES:
AND HE RECEIVED SIGHT FORTHWITH, AND AROSE, AND WAS BAPTIZED.
ACTS 9:18

PETER HAS A VISION

AND WHEN SAUL WAS COME TO JERUSALEM, HE ASSAYED TO JOIN HIMSELF TO THE DISCIPLES: BUT THEY WERE ALL AFRAID OF HIM, AND BELIEVED NOT THAT HE WAS A DISCIPLE.   ACTS 9:26

PAUL, THE NEW CHRISTIAN, TRAVELS TO JERUSALEM. THE DISCIPLES FEAR HIM.

PAUL IS ACCEPTED, AND THEY TALK OF THEIR PLANS FOR THE CHURCH.

AND SAW HEAVEN OPENED, AND A CERTAIN VESSEL DESCENDING UNTO HIM, AS IT HAD BEEN A GREAT SHEET KNIT AT THE FOUR CORNERS, AND LET DOWN TO THE EARTH. ACTS 10:11

CORNELIUS, A GODLY CENTURION, HAS A VISION.

CORNELIUS, YOUR OFFERINGS TO THE POOR HAVE PLEASED GOD. NOW, SEND FOR A MAN NAMED SIMON PETER.

AS THREE MEN TRAVEL TO FIND PETER, PETER ALSO HAS A VISION.

A SHEET COMING DOWN FROM HEAVEN...HOLDING ALL KINDS OF FOOD.

KILL AND EAT, PETER!

MANY OF THE FOODS ON THE SHEET, PETER KNOWS, WOULD BE CONSIDERED IMPURE AND UNFIT ACCORDING TO HEBREW LAW.

Peter Has a Vision - Acts 9

... OF A TRUTH I PERCEIVE THAT GOD IS NO RESPECTER OF PERSONS: BUT IN EVERY NATION HE THAT FEARETH HIM, AND WORKETH RIGHTEOUSNESS, IS ACCEPTED WITH HIM.   ACTS 10:34-35

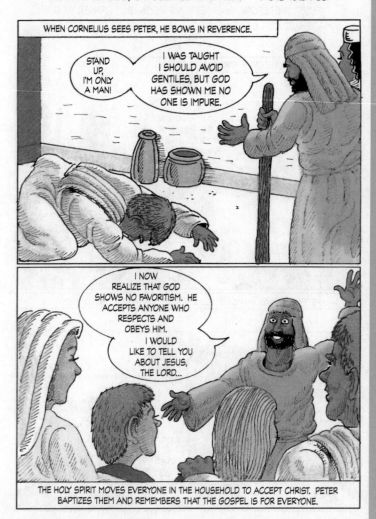

Peter Has a Vision - Acts 9

PETER AND THE ANGEL

PETER THEREFORE WAS KEPT IN PRISON: BUT PRAYER WAS
MADE WITHOUT CEASING OF THE CHURCH UNTO GOD FOR HIM.
ACTS 12:5

AND, BEHOLD, THE ANGEL OF THE LORD CAME UPON HIM, AND A LIGHT SHINED IN THE PRISON: AND HE SMOTE PETER ON THE SIDE, AND RAISED HIM UP.   ACTS 12:7

Peter and the Angel - Acts 12

WHEN THEY WERE PAST THE FIRST AND THE SECOND WARD, THEY CAME UNTO
THE IRON GATE THAT LEADETH UNTO THE CITY; WHICH OPENED TO THEM
OF HIS OWN ACCORD .... ACTS 12:10

Peter and the Angel - Acts 12

BUT PETER CONTINUED KNOCKING: AND WHEN THEY HAD OPENED THE DOOR, AND SAW HIM, THEY WERE ASTONISHED.   ACTS 12:16

Peter and the Angel - Acts 12

237

PAUL'S FIRST JOURNEY

AS THEY MINISTERED TO THE LORD, AND FASTED, THE HOLY GHOST SAID, SEPARATE ME BARNABAS AND SAUL FOR THE WORK WHEREUNTO I HAVE CALLED THEM.   ACTS 13:2

THE HOLY SPIRIT SAYS TO THE CHRISTIANS AT ANTIOCH: "SET APART BARNABAS AND PAUL FOR THE WORK TO WHICH I HAVE CALLED THEM." THE CHURCH FASTS, PRAYS, THEN LAYS HANDS ON THESE TWO.

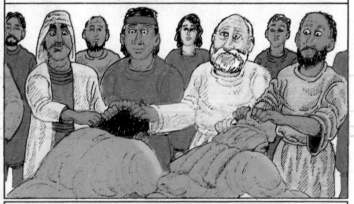

THE CHURCH IS SENDING OUT THE FIRST MISSIONARIES.

FOR SO HATH THE LORD COMMANDED US, SAYING, I HAVE SET THEE TO BE A LIGHT OF THE GENTILES, THAT THOU SHOULDEST BE FOR SALVATION UNTO THE ENDS OF THE EARTH.   ACTS 13:47

AND WHEN THE GENTILES HEARD THIS, THEY WERE GLAD, AND
GLORIFIED THE WORD OF THE LORD: AND AS MANY AS WERE ORDAINED
TO ETERNAL LIFE BELIEVED.   ACTS 13:48

THE GENTILES ACCEPT PAUL'S PREACHING GLADLY, AND BEGIN STARTING CHURCHES.
BUT JEWISH LEADERS MAKE TROUBLE, AND THE TWO GO TO THE NEXT CITY.

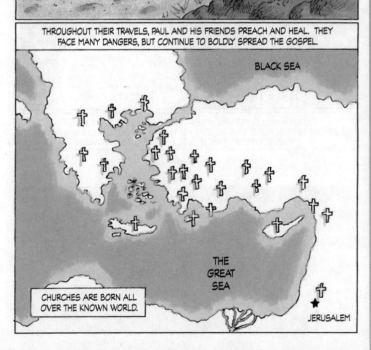

THROUGHOUT THEIR TRAVELS, PAUL AND HIS FRIENDS PREACH AND HEAL. THEY
FACE MANY DANGERS, BUT CONTINUE TO BOLDLY SPREAD THE GOSPEL.

BLACK SEA

THE
GREAT
SEA

CHURCHES ARE BORN ALL
OVER THE KNOWN WORLD.

JERUSALEM

Paul's First Journey - Acts 13

PAUL'S SHIPWRECK

AND WHEN IT WAS DETERMINED THAT WE SHOULD SAIL INTO ITALY, THEY
DELIVERED PAUL AND CERTAIN OTHER PRISONERS UNTO ONE NAMED
JULIUS, A CENTURION OF AUGUSTUS' BAND.   ACTS 27:1

PAUL APPEARS BEFORE AGRIPPA. BUT INSTEAD OF DEFENDING HIMSELF, HE
WITNESSES FOR CHRIST.

DO YOU THINK YOU CAN TALK
A KING INTO BEING A CHRISTIAN
WITH A FEW WORDS?

I ONLY WISH
YOU AND EVERYONE
HERE COULD BECOME
WHAT I AM — EXCEPT
FOR THE CHAINS!

AGRIPPA WOULD SET PAUL FREE — BUT PAUL HAS ASKED TO APPEAR
BEFORE NERO, IN ROME. THIS ALLOWS HIM TO TAKE THE GOSPEL TO THE WORLD'S
GREATEST CITY. SO PAUL IS PUT ON A SHIP BOUND FOR ROME.

AND NOW I EXHORT YOU TO BE OF GOOD CHEER: FOR THERE SHALL BE
NO LOSS OF ANY MAN'S LIFE AMONG YOU, BUT OF THE SHIP.
ACTS 27:22

AND THE REST, SOME ON BOARDS, AND SOME ON BROKEN PIECES OF THE SHIP. AND SO IT CAME TO PASS, THAT THEY ESCAPED ALL SAFE TO LAND.   ACTS 27:44

Paul's Shipwreck - Acts 27

AND PAUL DWELT TWO WHOLE YEARS IN HIS OWN HIRED HOUSE
... PREACHING THE KINGDOM OF GOD, AND TEACHING THOSE THINGS
WHICH CONCERN THE LORD JESUS CHRIST ....   ACTS 28:30-31

PAUL BUILDS A FIRE FOR WARMTH. THE HEAT ATTRACTS A SNAKE, WHICH BITES PAUL'S HAND. THE OTHERS SEE IT AS A SIGN FROM GOD.

LOOK! GOD MUST WANT THE PRISONER KILLED AFTER ALL!

BUT THE BITE HAS NO EFFECT ON PAUL — SO NOW THE MEN THINK HE IS A GOD. PAUL AND THE OTHERS ARE TAKEN TO A HOME NEARBY WHERE PAUL HEALS THE OWNER'S SICK FATHER.

THIS PAUL CAN DO ANYTHING!

AFTER WINTER, THE CREW AND PRISONERS SAIL AGAIN IN A NEW SHIP. PAUL IS A PRISONER IN ROME — YET HE CONTINUES TO PREACH THE GOSPEL AND CHANGE THE WORLD.

Paul's Shipwreck - Acts 27

THE MINISTRY OF PAUL

AND THERE CAME THITHER CERTAIN JEWS FROM ANTIOCH AND ICONIUM, WHO PERSUADED THE PEOPLE, AND, HAVING STONED PAUL, DREW HIM OUT OF THE CITY.   ACTS 14:19

THE BOOK OF ACTS TELLS OF PAUL'S MISSIONARY JOURNEYS. HE HAS MANY ADVENTURES. CLEVERLY, HE SPEAKS TO PEOPLE USING THEIR OWN IDEAS.

YOU GREEKS HAVE STATUES FOR ALL THE GODS — EVEN AN "UNKNOWN GOD!" I'M HERE TO TELL YOU WHO THAT UNKNOWN GOD IS...

SOMETIMES HIS WORDS MAKE PEOPLE ANGRY. ON ONE OCCASION, HE IS ALMOST KILLED BY STONING.

THEN THE DISCIPLES TOOK HIM BY NIGHT, AND LET HIM DOWN BY THE WALL IN A BASKET.   ACTS 9:25

ANOTHER TIME, PAUL FINDS OUT ABOUT A PLOT TO KILL HIM. FRIENDS HELP HIM ESCAPE IN A BASKET, LOWERED THROUGH A HOLE IN THE CITY WALL.

HE IS OFTEN ACCUSED AND BROUGHT TO TRIAL BEFORE THE ROMANS. HE TAKES THESE OPPORTUNITIES TO TALK ABOUT JESUS.

THAT IF THOU SHALT CONFESS WITH THY MOUTH THE LORD JESUS, AND SHALT BELIEVE IN THINE HEART THAT GOD HATH RAISED HIM FROM THE DEAD, THOU SHALT BE SAVED.   ROMANS 10:9

HE SPENDS MANY YEARS IN A ROMAN PRISON, AWAITING TRIAL. HE WRITES LETTERS — "EPISTLES" — TO CHURCHES AND FRIENDS IN MANY CITIES.

THE LETTER TO THE ROMANS TELLS HOW, BECAUSE OF OUR SIN, WE COULD NEVER SAVE OURSELVES — BUT JESUS, WHO IS PERFECT, CAN SAVE US.

THE TWO LETTERS TO THE CORINTHIANS DEAL WITH THE ARGUMENTS AND IMMATURITY OF THE CHURCH AT CORINTH. PAUL EXPLAINS HOW LOVE IS GOD'S GREATEST GIFT.

PAUL TELLS THE GALATIANS ABOUT THE FRUIT OF THE SPIRIT: LOVE, JOY, PEACE, PATIENCE, KINDNESS, GOODNESS, FAITHFULNESS, GENTLENESS, AND SELF-CONTROL.

EPHESIANS AND COLOSSIANS TELL ABOUT UNITY IN THE CHURCH — AND IN THE FAMILY.

AND HAVING THIS CONFIDENCE, I KNOW THAT I SHALL ABIDE AND
CONTINUE WITH YOU ALL FOR YOUR FURTHERANCE AND JOY OF FAITH.
PHILIPPIANS 1:25

THE OTHER CHURCHES SHARE PAUL'S LETTERS, COPYING THEM AND PASSING THEM ON.

PHILIPPIANS SPEAKS OF JOY IN CHRIST — A JOY WE CAN HAVE NO MATTER WHAT HAPPENS IN LIFE.

HE TELLS THE THESSALONIANS TO STAND FIRM IN TOUGH TIMES. AFTER ALL, WE NEVER KNOW WHEN THE LORD WILL RETURN!

PAUL DIRECTS HIS YOUNG FRIENDS TIMOTHY AND TITUS ON WHAT KINDS OF LEADERS THE CHURCH SHOULD HAVE. PHILEMON TELLS OF FORGIVENESS.

PAUL'S WORDS HELP US BUILD STRONG CHURCHES AND CHRISTIANS.

The Ministry of Paul - Acts and Paul's Letters

LETTERS FOR LIVING

SIMON PETER, A SERVANT AND AN APOSTLE OF JESUS CHRIST, TO THEM THAT HAVE OBTAINED LIKE PRECIOUS FAITH WITH US THROUGH THE RIGHTEOUSNESS OF GOD AND OUR SAVIOUR JESUS CHRIST.

2 PETER 1:1

DURING THE FIRST CENTURY, THE YOUNG CHURCHES SEEK TO APPLY JESUS' TEACHINGS TO LIFE. PAUL AND THE OTHER APOSTLES OFFER GUIDANCE AND ENCOURAGEMENT IN LETTERS SHARED AMONG THE CHURCHES.

WE'VE RECEIVED ANOTHER LETTER FROM PETER! HE HAS ANSWERED SOME OF OUR QUESTIONS.

THESE CHURCHES ARE SMALL AND SIMPLE, MEETING IN BELIEVERS' HOMES.

THE LETTER TO THE HEBREWS HAS THIS MESSAGE: LIFE IS DIFFICULT, BUT KEEP THE FAITH! REMEMBER THE FAITH HEROES OF THE PAST — ABRAHAM, MOSES, AND ALL THE OTHERS.

BUT BE YE DOERS OF THE WORD, AND NOT HEARERS ONLY, DECEIVING YOUR OWN SELVES.   JAMES 1:22

THE LETTER FROM <u>JAMES</u>, THE BROTHER OF JESUS, REMINDS US TO BE A DOER OF GOD'S WORD, NOT JUST A HEARER. FAITH WITHOUT ACTION IS WORTHLESS. WE SHOW OUR FAITH IN CARING FOR WIDOWS AND ORPHANS, AND CONTROLLING OUR SPEECH.

<u>PETER</u>, THE APOSTLE, IS THE AUTHOR OF TWO LETTERS. PETER ENCOURAGES PERSECUTED BELIEVERS TO BE HOLY. IT IS AN HONOR TO SUFFER FOR CHRIST.

BUT IF WE WALK IN THE LIGHT, AS HE IS IN THE LIGHT, WE HAVE FELLOWSHIP ONE WITH ANOTHER, AND THE BLOOD OF JESUS CHRIST HIS SON CLEANSETH US FROM ALL SIN.   1 JOHN 1:7

JUDE WRITES THAT WE SHOULD BE SERIOUS ABOUT CHRISTIAN TEACHING, AVOIDING THE IDEAS OF GODLESS PEOPLE.

JOHN, THE BELOVED DISCIPLE, IS THE AUTHOR OF A GOSPEL, THREE LETTERS, AND REVELATION. HIS BEAUTIFUL LETTERS TEACH US TO WALK IN THE LIGHT, AND TO LOVE ONE ANOTHER. WE ARE THE CHILDREN OF GOD.

AND GOD SHALL WIPE AWAY ALL TEARS FROM THEIR EYES; AND THERE
SHALL BE NO MORE DEATH, NEITHER SORROW, NOR CRYING, NEITHER
SHALL THERE BE ANY MORE PAIN . . . .   REVELATION 21:4

THE WORLD OF GENESIS

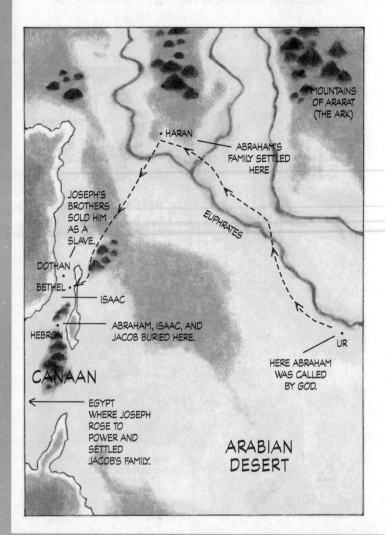

MOUNTAINS OF ARARAT (THE ARK)

HARAN

ABRAHAM'S FAMILY SETTLED HERE

EUPHRATES

JOSEPH'S BROTHERS SOLD HIM AS A SLAVE.

DOTHAN

BETHEL

ISAAC

ABRAHAM, ISAAC, AND JACOB BURIED HERE.

HEBRON

UR

HERE ABRAHAM WAS CALLED BY GOD.

CANAAN

EGYPT WHERE JOSEPH ROSE TO POWER AND SETTLED JACOB'S FAMILY.

ARABIAN DESERT

MOSES AND THE EXODUS

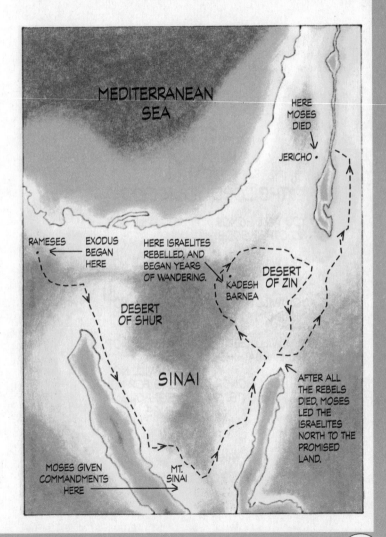

MEDITERRANEAN SEA

HERE MOSES DIED

JERICHO •

RAMESES • ← EXODUS BEGAN HERE

HERE ISRAELITES REBELLED, AND BEGAN YEARS OF WANDERING.

• KADESH BARNEA

DESERT OF ZIN

DESERT OF SHUR

SINAI

AFTER ALL THE REBELS DIED, MOSES LED THE ISRAELITES NORTH TO THE PROMISED LAND.

MOSES GIVEN COMMANDMENTS HERE →

MT. SINAI

I AM
THE LORD YOUR GOD:

YOU WILL HONOR
NO OTHER GODS.

YOU WILL MAKE
NO IDOLS.

YOU WILL NOT
MISUSE MY NAME.

YOU WILL KEEP
THE SABBATH HOLY.

YOU WILL HONOR
YOUR PARENTS.

YOU WILL NOT
KILL.

YOU WILL NOT
COMMIT ADULTERY.

YOU WILL NOT
STEAL.

YOU WILL NOT LIE.

YOU WILL NOT
LONG FOR YOUR
NEIGHBORS
THINGS.

FAMILY LIFE IN ISRAEL

BABY COULD BE KEPT IN A SIMPLE HAMMOCK.

DAUGHTERS HELPED MOTHER IN THE HOME UNTIL MARRIAGE.

AT AGE FIVE, SONS BEGAN TO BE TAUGHT A CRAFT BY FATHERS—SUCH AS WOODWORK, AND DUTIES OF RELIGION.

WATER

SPINNING

GRAIN BASKET

OIL

BRICKS, CLAY AND MUD MADE SIMPLE HOMES, ROOFS WERE USED FOR ACTIVITIES.

THE 23RD PSALM

The Lord is my shepherd;
I shall not want. He maketh me to
lie down in green pastures:
he leadeth me beside the still waters.
He restoreth my soul: he leadeth me in the
paths of righteousness for his name's sake.
Yea, though I walk through the valley of the
shadow of death, I will fear no evil:
for thou art with me; thy rod and thy staff
they comfort me. Thou preparest a table
before me in the presence of mine enemies:
thou anointest my head with oil; my cup
runneth over. Surely goodness and mercy
shall follow me all the days
of my life: and I will dwell
in the house of the Lord
for ever.

SHEPHERDS AND FISHERMEN

WATER.

STAFF FOR CLIMBING, HERDING.

LEATHER BAG.

DAVID AND MOSES WERE TWO OF THE BIBLE'S SHEPHERDS. KEEPING SHEEP TOOK TRAINING AND DEDICATION. A SHEPHERD KNEW EACH OF HIS SHEEP WELL. AND THEY KNEW AND ANSWERED ONLY HIS VOICE, HE WOULD RISK HIS LIFE TO RESCUE A SHEEP FROM A CLIFF OR WILD ANIMAL. JESUS IS OUR "GOOD SHEPHERD."

JESUS SAID; "I WILL MAKE YOU FISHERS OF MEN." MATTHEW 4:19

FISHERMEN CAST THEIR NETS IN HOPE OF A BOUNTY OF FISH FOR THE MARKET. FISHING WAS OFTEN DONE AT NIGHT WITH TORCHLIGHT. IT WAS HARD LABOR.

SOLDIERS IN BIBLE TIMES

A SOLDIER OFTEN WORE A CUIRASS WITH METAL SCALES.

PHILISTINES WORE FEATHERED HELMETS.

ARMOR WAS FIRST CREATED WHEN BOWS BECAME MORE POWERFUL, FIRING ARROWS 300 YARDS OR MORE.

SPEARS WERE USED FOR CLOSE COMBAT

EARLY ARROW HEADS WERE WOODEN, BUT LATER ONES WERE BONE, BRONZE, OR IRON.

THIS ANCIENT DRAWING SHOWS TWO ARCHERS BEHIND A FULL-BODY SHIELD.

ARROWS COULD BE DIPPED IN POISON OR SET ON FIRE, THEN SHOT.

THE LIFE OF JESUS

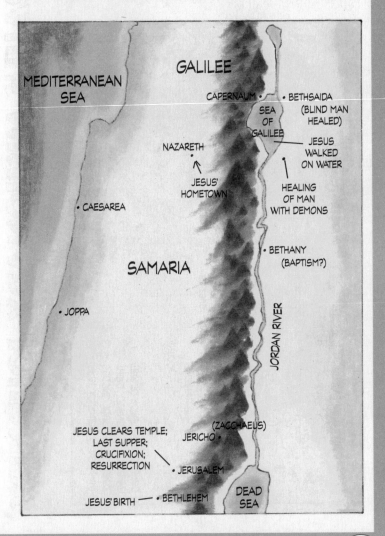

MEDITERRANEAN
SEA

GALILEE

CAPERNAUM • • BETHSAIDA
(BLIND MAN
HEALED)

SEA
OF
GALILEE

JESUS
WALKED
ON WATER

NAZARETH
•
↑
JESUS'
HOMETOWN

HEALING
OF MAN
WITH DEMONS

• CAESAREA

SAMARIA

• BETHANY
(BAPTISM?)

• JOPPA

JORDAN RIVER

JESUS CLEARS TEMPLE;
LAST SUPPER;
CRUCIFIXION;
RESURRECTION

(ZACCHAEUS)
JERICHO •

• JERUSALEM

JESUS' BIRTH — • BETHLEHEM

DEAD
SEA

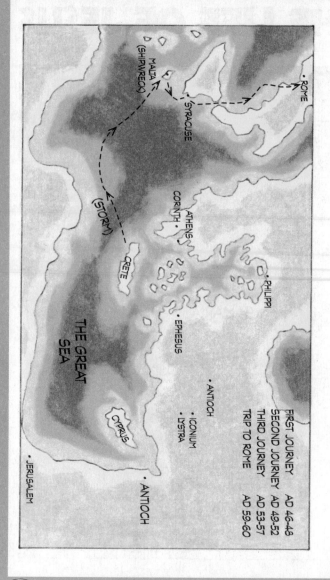

PAUL'S MISSIONARY JOURNEYS

- ROME

- SYRACUSE

MALTA
(SHIPWRECK)

(STORM)

CORINTH •
• ATHENS

CRETE

• PHILIPPI

THE GREAT
SEA

• EPHESUS

• ANTIOCH
• ICONIUM
• LYSTRA

CYPRUS

• ANTIOCH

• JERUSALEM

FIRST JOURNEY   AD 46-48
SECOND JOURNEY   AD 49-52
THIRD JOURNEY   AD 53-57
TRIP TO ROME   AD 59-60

VERSES TO KNOW

For God so loved the world, that he gave his only begotten Son, that whosoever believeth in him should not perish, but have everlasting life. John 3:16

Love one another.   1 John 4:7

All scripture is given by inspiration of God, and is profitable for doctrine, for reproof, for correction, for   instruction in righteousness.   2 Timothy 3:16

Children, obey your parents in the Lord, for this is right. Ephesians 6:1

Thou shalt love the Lord thy God with all thy heart, and with all thy soul, and with all thy strength, and with all thy mind; and thy neighbour as thyself.   Luke 10:27

Trust in the LORD with all thine heart; and lean not unto thine own understanding. In all thy ways acknowledge him, and he shall direct thy paths.   Proverbs 3: 5,6

The grass withereth, and the flower fadeth: but the word of our God shall stand for ever.   Isaiah 40:8

Rob Suggs keeps busy as a full-time freelance author and illustrator. His entertaining titles include *It Came from Beneath the Pew, Preacher from the Black Lagoon, Murphy Goes to Church,* and *The Adventures of Brother Biddle.* Rob shares his home in Atlanta, Georgia, with his wife, two children, and a 200 pound cat.

Christopher Gray is an illustrator and writer and owner of Scribble Boy Studios, a company dedicated to producing quality books for children. For the past eleven years he has worked in television, magazine, and corporate advertising, creating identities for several major corporations. Christopher, his wife, Kristine, and their two children, live in Carol Stream, Illinois.